911, BROKEN.
GIVE IT TO GOD!

911, BROKEN.
GIVE IT TO GOD!

Taking the right steps to overcome the battle with Autism & Addiction

GAIL CLARK

XULON ELITE

Xulon Press
555 Winderley Pl, Suite 225
Maitland, FL 32751
407.339.4217
www.xulonpress.com

© 2023 by Gail Clark

All rights reserved solely by the author. The author guarantees all contents are original and do not infringe upon the legal rights of any other person or work. No part of this book may be reproduced in any form without the permission of the author.

Due to the changing nature of the Internet, if there are any web addresses, links, or URLs included in this manuscript, these may have been altered and may no longer be accessible. The views and opinions shared in this book belong solely to the author and do not necessarily reflect those of the publisher. The publisher therefore disclaims responsibility for the views or opinions expressed within the work.

Unless otherwise indicated, Scripture quotations taken from the New King James Version (NKJV). Copyright © 1982 by Thomas Nelson, Inc. Used by permission. All rights reserved.

Paperback ISBN-13: 978-1-66288-518-1
Ebook ISBN-13: 978-1-66288-519-8

Introduction

This is a true story about the emotional roller coaster of a single parent and the ups and downs of raising a child with the horrific disease of Autism, having to cope with everyday life and the difficulties that come about with the disease. Not to mention my substance abuse as well as trying to escape the pain and hurt and attacks of the enemy. I was battling a living hell. My son was facing depression, bullying, isolation, being ostracized and neglected, and I was on the ride with him. Then, we overcame a lot of those obstacles (with the help of the Lord!) even though all odds are against you (now that's Jesus!) and gaining back confidence. Feeling broken and torn down by some of your peers, and people in the school system as well. When being told you can't do something right, or anything right for that matter, proving them wrong later. What do you do when all hope has been taken away and you're broken and the demon of suicide is talking to you, telling you this is your only way out? Seems like a 911 moment to me, but God steps in when you least expect it, and turns what the devil meant for evil (and for what you thought was a lost cause) around to something you couldn't believe yourself, could turn out for good. Just remember, people like us need a voice, someone to hear our cry before it's too late, and Jesus is that voice! Sometimes I have to remind myself of these words "He'll never leave you or forsake you".

Table of Contents

1. Diagnosis & Characteristics of Autism......................1

2. Bullying & Addiction 9

3. I.E.P. Meetings & Tantrums 17

4. Triggers....................................... 23

5. More Tantrums.................................. 29

6. I.E.P. Meetings & Suicide Scares 35

7. Attorney Drops Ball & 911....................... 45

8. The Therapist & Much Prayer..................... 51

9. No Child Left Behind............................ 59

10. New Psychiatrist & Harmful Meds............... 69

11. The Pastor on Fire for Jesus! 73

12. The Case & The Psychologist 75

13. First Fruit Offerings............................ 81

14. Flare Ups & Apologies 83

15. Superior Court 85

16. Thanksgiving Holiday.......................... 89

17. The Nativity Story 97

18. Out of Control, give it to God! 99

19. Side Effects with the Meds..................... 105

20. Rose Bowl & Cable Company Issues 109

21. Life Skills Teacher & Blow Ups 115

22. Covid & The Key in the Bible Box 119

23. The Battle. 125

24. The Graduation 133

25. Effects of Covid 139

26. Spiritual Warfare & Broken 147

27. Hope. 149

28. The Power of God's Word! 155

Acknowledgements

I'd like to give thanks to some of the people that helped mold and shape me into the person I am today. These people have had a big influence on my life by inspiring me to even want to write. First, I'd like to give thanks to my Lord and Savior, Jesus Christ for never leaving or forsaking me. He stuck closer than a brother to me, He is King of Kings and Lord of Lords! I'd also like to thank my Pastor and his wife at Epicenter for my walk in Christ and guidance and growth in the Lord. I'd also like to thank my mother for her encouragement, my dad and his wife for their involvement in helping me on this project, especially my dad for always reassuring me I could do it and let me not forget my son, the main character in the book, for the impact and emotional tie in compelling me to write the book.

I would also like to thank all the T.V. stations Ministers and the different ministries that I would listen to, that fed me the Word of God that helped cleanse my mind, and soul and focused me.

T.B.N., Daystar, Impact, Larry Huch Ministries, Joyce Meyer's Ministry, Sid Roth, Discovering the Jewish Jesus Ministry, Jewish Voice, Creflo Dollar Ministry, Rod Parsley, Charles Stanly, Paula White, Jesse Duplantis, Ever-Increasing Faith Ministry, Maldonado Ministry, Life Outreach, Sarah Jakes Roberts, Jentezen Franklin, Ron Carpenter, Joel Osteen, Joseph Prince and Rabbi Cahn. I can't forget my beautiful daughter and my smart and beautiful grandchildren that give me the will to move forward and don't look back. Thank you all again, God Bless You!

CHAPTER 1:

The Diagnosis & Characteristics of Autism

This all began in 2001 on January 20th when George W. Bush became our 43rd United States President and on January 20th of the same year Dick Cheney was elected our 46th Vice President for the United States. On June 5th flooding in Houston, Texas from the Tropical Storm Allison took place, and we'll never forget on September 11th, the horrific attacks on 9/11 that were done to our World Trade Centers in New York as well as the Afghanistan War on October 7, 2001. The devil was busy, one good thing that came out of all this turmoil was that my precious baby boy was born on August 8th, 2001. We will just call him Xman to protect the innocent.

In sunny Pasadena, California, when he was between four-six months old, he was doing just fine. He was lively, very energetic, he loved to make little noises while standing up in his crib holding the bars. He had a duck that sang the "old McDonald had a farm, e, i, e, i, o song". We have all sang that song, those of us that know it and if you want to know what it sounds like, you can Google it. He would quack along to the song, so cute. After he was around eight months old, we moved to Los Angeles, California. There I met my neighbor across the street, we will call her Ms. V., she had a Daycare. Ms. V. would watch Xman periodically when I had to run errands. While watching Xman she noticed that her little boy who was younger than mine was developing faster in gross and fine motor skills. She gave me an example of the way her little boy could grasp things and how Xman could not do the same while eating, such as holding a hot dog or something, etc. Ms. V. came to me one day and said that I need to get Xman a second opinion and have him diagnosed, she gave me a number to call, and I did. Now to some people this would have been a game changer and might not have received this information well. It could have started a war between the two parents but, Thank God! I didn't go there. I took it as she was only trying to help. I knew how much she loved kids. She was adopting two kids at the time, and she really cared about my son as well. I know one thing, God loved me and my son, and He wanted me to get my son help. I wanted what was best for my child and to nip this in the bud with the quickness! "Thank you, Lord". I made a call to a lady from the number Ms. V. gave me, and we set up an appointment and she came to my home. The lady gave me information on where to take my son after she did the assessment and tests on Xman, he did show signs of delay in his development in certain areas. I was informed to take him to Frank D. Lanterman's Regional Center in Los Angeles, California and they diagnosed Xman with Autism. This was my worst nightmare ever, but a blessing at the same time. I know you're wondering why I say a blessing as well. I'll tell you, because now I knew what the actual problem was that we were dealing with. The center also connected me with a lot of very helpful resources to be able to address this demon of Autism properly! and with the Lord's help, to nip this in the bud by the Blood of the Lamb. I remembered after his vaccinations that his behavior started to change, I had also done a little research on my own and some doctors in their information said the vaccinations could have caused the Autism due to high levels of mercury in the shots. I noticed tantrums started to flare up frequently, frustration, and he also stopped talking as much.

He had been talking and saying little words prior to the shots, words like mama, dada, hi, bye, and his sister's name, etc., then all of a sudden, he stopped, and the tantrums got worse. Watching your child revert to an infant all over again when I was seeing him progress was devastating to say the least, also, not knowing what to expect next along with this horrifying disease. It broke me, I started drinking, and wanting to numb myself. I went into depression. I didn't want to face the facts, at the same time I thought to myself I have to do whatever it takes to utilize all my options and help I could get for him. I thought, what kind of quality of life would my son have

The Diagnosis & Characteristics of Autism

if I didn't do all I could do. I didn't want to tell anyone about this yet, but I knew my family needed to know. I ended up moving in with my mother and put Xman in another daycare that I was referred to. They got me transportation and everything for him. He really liked the school. Christmas was coming up, my favorite time of the year, and the daycare was putting on a Christmas Program for the parents and my son, Xman was in it. He was going to play the drums on stage with a little band they had, so all the parents were invited to the show. I noticed while Xman was beating the drums, all of a sudden, he stopped and broke out in tears. I looked at him struggling, he seemed very disconnected, and in fear. I didn't know whether to jump up and grab him, would this make it worse, but I didn't want to leave him hanging so I nudged Xman's father, and he went and picked him up and calmed him down. The teacher also came over to speak with us about it, we all agreed it was a little too much for him, plus this was his first little program, I had to also be calm for Xman. You can't show too many panic signs, because it could trigger the child as well. It's hard being a parent and watching your child struggle like this.

I noticed that Xman didn't give any eye contact. If you called him by name, he wouldn't answer. You could go up to him and speak to him face to face and he would look down or around you, but never give you eye to eye contact. I took him to the doctor and had his hearing and eyes checked. They said everything was just fine, in actuality, they didn't understand his condition. Later on I found out that Autism can make a child disconnect from others, and also isolate themselves. At around two to four years old, I started noticing my son liking to bounce very hard on the bed with his body, hard enough that it worried me that he could hurt his back or neck, then he would run up close to the wall and you couldn't even put a coin between him and the wall. Then the noises started ("the noises"). I was waking up one morning and I heard this dolphin-like noise coming from his bedroom, so I ran into his room and there he was, Xman, jumping on the bed, making this dolphin-like sound and then every day after that for a long while he did this. I had my daughter with us who was a lot older than Xman helping me with him, she was very good with him. You could tell they really loved each other. I finally put my son in preschool down the street from my home, and I started working part time. I thought it's time to see if he can fit in with other kids his age and start learning the fundamentals that they teach and see if he could handle a class setting.

Now before that, I worked with him with counting numbers and alphabets, he would look at cartoons that were educational such as Sesame Street and others. He did pretty good, he would sing and count along. I knew I had to start working with him so he wouldn't be lost. When he did start school, after a while in the school I had put him in, I started getting phone calls at work telling me that he was throwing tantrums, spitting, etc. They got my son an Aide to work with him because they noticed when it was something Xman couldn't do, he got frustrated he would blow up. This is part of the disease of Autism, frustration. You need to have a lot of patience with these kids that I did not have at the time. The Lord knew what He was doing and how this would all play out. Sometimes the tantrums got so bad that I would have to leave work to pick him up and take off the rest of the day.

I ended up asking my boss if I could work from home. He said yes, for a while, but there were things that needed to be done at the job site that I couldn't do from home. My job was marketing and sales, to pull clients in, to buy from our store especially a lot of schools for sports activities and, set up appointments for the owner to show the samples of the different materials we had for whatever sport they wanted uniforms for. He needed to take them swatches to look at so that we could close the deals, but working from home didn't give me access to everything I needed to keep the operation working smoothly. There was a guy that I worked with, real closely for logos that go on the sportswear, that I needed to work with one on one at the store. Sadly, to say, my work ethics started to go downhill. I tried but I couldn't let them at the job down, so I quit.

I had to make a choice, my son or the job, and my son needed 100% of my attention and also professional help to be successful in life, and not lost or left behind, so you know as a mother which route I went of course, my son came before the job. Sometimes you do what's best whether you want to or not. God took the reins and started leading me in the right direction

The Diagnosis & Characteristics of Autism

for my son's help. I became my son's care provider because I couldn't work. My son got on disability, and we made headway uphill so that I got working on the progression of my son's quality of life. There's an old saying "crawl before you walk". We still had a long journey. I started seeking other facilities for my son's needs, I started with a group called Aces and CVRC which stands for Central Valley Regional Center. A young lady would come out once or twice a month to educate me on the disease and give me help by sending people to come work with my son in the home. Such as, helping him with gross and fine motor skills, with games, and Icons to refer to when he couldn't remember how to ask or what he should be doing. They would also play with him, like, playing ball, practice putting things in order, counting, stacking. The Icons would show him by pictures on what he needs to know and do next starting from morning to evening, also skills that would help him to verbalize better, and light social skills that would help him interact better. This all happened once a week, sometimes twice, and before the person helping left, she would go over everything she had done that day with me, and also kept a log of his reactions and progress. Then when she left, I would take over with the things she did to reinforce her work with him until he could do these activities on his own. It was a long haul, but it had to get done, and nothing was going to get in the way of it. The Icons were posted on the wall for him to see at all times as a reminder of what needed to be done every day such as washing your face, brushing teeth, doing hair, eating, going to the bathroom, etc. They even gave Xman samples of items to show how to tie shoes, zipping and snapping, buttoning, open, and closing samples. I noticed when he got frustrated, he would start throwing, kicking, and spitting, even breaking things, and crying. When he ate certain foods, he would feel the textures of them before eating them. At first, he was a picky eater. Now as time went on, I started taking him to a therapist that also would give him strategic things to play with and do things such as lining up items, counting, pronouncing small words, rolling, stacking tasks, and working with his speech. Autistic kids can be repetitive, that's part of the disease. Repeating things over and over, and getting stuck on a subject, and not being able to move on, so, that needed to be addressed. I can remember the potty-training days, difficult is not even the word for it. It was so challenging.

Out of frustration, when at school, he'd see other kids playing, he would isolate himself, another trait of theirs. No mother wants to hear that their child doesn't want to socialize with other children, and just be alone all the time, that really broke me when I was told that's how a lot of them are, and no one could guarantee me when he would ever come out of this shell. I went through crying spells, and depression several nights in the process. One thing I can say is that he loved the water, we both did. We had a pool at the time, a nine-footer, inground, and he showed no fear of it at all. Matter of fact, that was his comfort zone. He didn't mind getting his face wet, dunking, and jumping off the diving board was his thing. His father taught him how to swim, he loved to dog paddle, play with items such as water guns, balls, and so on. After a while he started swimming underwater learning strokes, he was great at it, and I was very proud. His father did teach him a lot of is swimming skills. Thank God!

As Xman went on to the first grade, he remained in Special Education. He had a young teacher in her 20's that worked well with him, we will call her Mrs. B. She saw his potential and gave us hope. She started working with him in math and reading light stuff, she brought out the best in him. I was so glad to have her, because I saw a lot of other teachers and aides that seemed to be like babysitters only, and if a child started to stim, meaning doing little repetitive things such as rocking, blinking, bouncing, etc., or being defiant, some didn't bother to take the time in helping with that child, but Mrs. B. was very patient and super caring. She was up for the task and faced the challenge head on. I saw him accepting the challenge and getting interested in learning, although he still had tantrums and other issues. There was a lot of nights I stayed up late worried and full of anxiety. There's nothing worse than not knowing what to do for your child. Anyone who has a child with a disability is always concerned or should be about the quality of life their child will have later in life. Like, can they fend for themselves if something was to happen like an emergency or God forbid, something was to happen to their parents. Who would help out? How will they be treated by others?

The Diagnosis & Characteristics of Autism

How will they be able to deal with real issues? Will they ever be able to have a family of their own? Being able to communicate without being mocked and, enough money to survive? Friends and support are some of the main things that are important, and to be able to differentiate between friends and associates or impostors just playing the role to take advantage of them, these are just a few of the issues they'll be dealing with. It's crucial to teach the child the difference, so they could determine on their own. Also, Life skills on how to navigate, manners. Praying that they use common sense, there's grooming, hygiene. My son always asks me about how he'll survive if he was on his own. I told him everything will be alright with the help of the Lord and me, getting the support he needs, he'll be just fine, you must reassure them.

CHAPTER 2:

Bullying & Addiction

I had him read through the Bible during the week. The Bible strengthens him in his walk of life, and he has come a long way. That's our manual to life. It gives instruction on what to do in circumstances that even I don't know how to explain or show my son. That's one reason why he's growing mentally. Xman is still human, and as we all know will be going through trials and tribulations while on this earth, but with prayer, he'll be just fine. Xman's not perfect, no one is, and all of us need the right guidance and direction, and we get this through the Word of God.

Xman was also being bullied in school, it was a very hard time for the both of us. I had meeting after meeting at his school with his teachers, and with the staff members, some acted on it and then there were some who didn't care. You would think that under the circumstances they would be more concerned, but not always. I would call an emergency meeting when I would find out these things and come to find out that sometimes it would be the teacher that had the issues with Xman. What do you do when a child is getting treated differently because of his condition, it's just not a pretty sight. A lot of nights I'd find myself waking up crying, and also having a lot of anxiety. I started drinking and getting back into old bad habits, going around with the wrong people, taking the wrong advice, and going in the wrong direction. I found myself confused at times trying to juggle bills, and everything else. Xman had anger problems, because of his problems at school, they started getting out of control. A couple of his teachers really made his life a living hell. He started lashing out on me because of what happened at

9

911, Broken. **Give it to God!**

school, and then it could be his electronics not working or he couldn't find things. It would lead him and I getting in arguments, then he would run up to me, I would try to be cool, but it would only escalate into a bad blow up where he might grab a knife and try to cut himself. I would be crying and trying to tell him there's another way to deal with this, not suicide. He would hit me or the wall, I've got about eight holes in my walls, and I just moved here. I didn't really want to tell anybody, but then I thought maybe venting would help relieve the stress. You have to understand there is a disconnect in these children, and teens, and young adults with this disease, they don't process stuff the same unless God heals them. That's why, when they get angry, they could possibly kill somebody, being parents, or someone else, easy. After it happened, down the road, they might be remorseful, but it could be too late. The brain functioning is very different. This is why you need Jesus! One doctor said that the back of the brain is not as fully developed as the front of the brain. I can see that being true, because of the violent behavior I've experienced, once they get started, it's hard to get them back in control. So, unless you've lived with a child that has these traits you can't tell me nothing, because you never know from day to day what it will be like. All I know is I'm a believer in the Lord, and if it weren't for prayer, I could have been dead, or I could have hurt my own child trying to defend myself. It's no joke. As they get older, bigger, and stronger it can get worst. I know most Autistic kids, teens, don't like change, they like routine and that's a big trigger when change might come about, like for instance, moving and changing friends, if they have any, because they like to isolate, a lot of them. It could be a new haircut, losing the remote control, etc. I remember I was on the phone with our cable television company because the television wouldn't come on, it was a message on there, and it said to check the plugs, reset if that didn't work, and call them, so I had to call them. My son's temper hit the ceiling. I knew this was going to be a blow up, he started throwing stuff, breaking stuff, using profanity when the people on the line from the cable company could hear him. I was so embarrassed, but I also wanted them to know how serious this was for me to get this working again. I was on the phone for an hour and a half trying to work under these conditions while trying to get

Bullying & Addiction

the TV to work. I started crying, I woke up to my son on a weekend finally being able to sleep a little later, but couldn't because of this, I was beside myself. Finally, the lady on the phone said she would send out a technician with no charge, she heard my son in the background going through the motions and had mercy on me. That's what I mean about prayer, when you think the Lord has forgotten about you, He hasn't, thank God!

My son is now in high school, first day of high school had started back. I made sure to go to church that Sunday before school began, because I knew that if I stay close to the Lord, and in His Word, everything will fall in place. The message was about eliminating the wrong people in your life, because who you hang out with is who can mold you, and can also have an effect on your thought process and if you're not into Jesus they'll make wrong decisions. Like the Pastor said, "going back to your old vomit". The first day was a beautiful day for me and my son, also for my daughter and her kids. My son got "good" classes; he came back happy unlike before during last year. It was a nightmare! He had gone through so much drama with the teachers, class bullying and more. I have to stay in prayer always, for me and my family at all times because the devil comes through people, places, things, also thoughts and so on. So, I've learned prayer works.

My daughter on the same day that Xman went back to school got a new job, a good one, God is awesome! She was also having transportation problems, but so happened that one of her acquaintances got the job also where my daughter would be working, both of their kids go to the same school so they can travel together to work, and also pick up the kids at the same place at school. God worked out a miracle on her behalf as well. When my son got home from school that day, he was so happy. He said to me he had a great day; we hadn't seen him so happy in a long time. His confidence was up, and very motivated. The year before, like I said, was pure hell! He's now in the 11th grade, a Junior. I just spoke with his developmental teacher, he's new too and I need to remind him of my son's ID and other things that he needs prompting on. Such as turning in homework, making sure he gets in his assignments on time, that I'm to be notified, and to make sure he makes up any missing assignments, so he doesn't fall behind like last year.

His algebra teacher and aide dropped the ball last year and didn't let him know about his missing assignments until the day before school was out. First, they said three assignments were missing, then they came up with this story that eight were missing, and were going to give him all zeros. But when I told them why did you wait until the closing of the school year, and questioning them and their ability as Special Education teachers, I was so upset to say the least. You can rest for sure they had to come correct, or all hell was going to break loose, because I intended to report all of this to their superiors! As a parent, you must stay involved with any and everything that their child is doing so that the child is not left behind. It's not a question, it's a fact, if you want to get the right results, prayer works. I try to keep my son reading the Bible like myself every morning except on Sunday when we go to church. That's the only thing that has kept me and him together. My daughter is grown with a family of her own, I tell her to read the Word of God also and go to church. In this day and age, it's not a joke, too much is going on in this crazy world we live in, man has messed it up, the devil is out of control. He's out to kill, steal and destroy, so we must stay focused and close to the Lord, none of us are perfect, no not one, but when the going gets tough you must refer to the Word of the Lord. He's the only for sure thing in our life we have to depend on. He always comes through, maybe not when you want something on your time, but He's always on time! If you wait on His timing, it's right on time, His mercy, and grace has carried me so far from anything I could ask or do for myself. Now as a single parent raising a son with Autism, my child has overcome so many obstacles, because God's given me the strength even when I thought I couldn't go any further in this situation.

Last night was Back-To-School Night for my son. I went and got a chance to speak with all but one of his teachers, seems like this could be a better year than the last one, we'll see. The teachers seem to have more compassion for the students this time than last year when I went to it. Last year was a disaster, his algebra teacher Mr. L. used to sing loud in the classroom and play loud music while the kids were trying to concentrate on their work. It's already hard enough because it's algebra, they need quiet

Bullying & Addiction

time to be able to process this kind of math. You would think as a teacher he would have known better, but no, and this was while doing their work. "Great job teacher"! The teacher Mr. L. also lied about it in the I.E.P. meeting which stands for Individual Educational Program, all Special Education kids have this, also in the meeting, Mr. L. said that he couldn't recall doing that, blaming it on my child's behavior etc. My son also told me that Mr. L. made comments to him to lower his self-esteem, and confidence. I had to get him a therapist behind all of this, and eventually, a psychiatrist. My child became withdrawn and felt ostracized, he also spoke of suicide due to mental trauma he experienced. When we had the I.E.P. meeting, I mentioned all of this, the teachers involved acted like it was no biggie, very nonchalant. I was ticked! After that I started looking to file a lawsuit against the school district to help not only my son, but others going through the same thing and to see it never happens to anyone else!

I called the Special Ed. Dept. to report it, they really didn't act concerned either. My son was always worried about "fitting in". "Quote-on-Quote" being normal as society says, he's conscious of his hair, his clothes, and wanting to just fit in. He likes challenges, tries to help himself, and be independent. I love that about him. I pray for him always to get treated fair. He has told me during school that people have called him retarded and weird, because of him trying to explain things when holding a conversation, or if they see him stimming occasionally. I told him if he can help it to really try and not let anyone see him stim, meaning the little gestures or things they do when they get excited or want to release stress etc... I knew to myself that it could be a problem if someone would see this behavior, these are Autistic traits. I believe that the stimming comes from anxiety or stress or trying to release extra energy that builds up in Autistic people. A lot of people with this disease have to take medication for it, but you don't know if the side effects in the medications could make it worse, and a lot of them are harmful to the body, they test out these drugs on these kids and adults because they're still doing research. Some of the drugs can do more harm than help, for example, they have lawsuits going on as we speak about a drug,

13

they give them, that cause the boys to grow breasts. You've probably seen it on TV, I don't want my child lethargic or dependent on these medications.

It's very obvious that when they stim, people will make fun of them or ask about it, and that can offend them. These are some of the trials and tribulations that we go through when dealing with this. He can get so frustrated behind a comment or something that he'll throw a tantrum when he gets home from school and starts hitting the walls, or trying to hurt himself by hitting himself or banging his head against the wall. He's even hit me before so hard in my eye that I was seeing a black like web to describe it, on the side of my eye that eventually went away, but it took a long time to leave my eye, it was very scary. My son is big and almost weighs close to 200 pounds and is tall. It's no joke. I picked up my son after school today, he was supposed to have his driver's training class but due to this crazy instructor that he had, they had to change his schedule. This guy was very aggressive with Xman, first, all of you have to remember he's never driven before. I'm speaking of my son, so the person in charge of driving needs to be very patient with him, right? Not screaming at him or falling asleep on my son while he's learning, expecting my son to know what to do next when this is all new to him. I don't know where they find these idiots but that's what this one was doing. Then, my son told me that he made him change seats with another boy in the car that was also new to this and learning, and when they changed seats for the other boy to drive the instructor completely calmed down with this guy. I couldn't wait to tell my son's dad about this, after all, my son's dad was paying for all of this. To give you a little insight, my son's dad and I have been broken up for a while now, that's it. I told Xman's dad about the driving news on how the instructor was acting toward our son. I called the owner of the company the next day, and my son's father went up there to the driving school. Oh, they apologized, you better believe it, because we don't play when it comes to something like this. They also gave us some free lessons, and also changed his instructor.

The next time Xman went, he had a new instructor that brought him home and told me he did pretty good. He just needed to practice his hand over hand turns and slowing down a little quicker. The instructor had

Bullying & Addiction

Xman drive down one of the main boulevards, and the instructor told me that Xman didn't do so bad, that let me know that it really was the other instructor, and that wasn't right. That's what I mean when I say you have to stay on top of the situation quickly and don't procrastinate with kids, teens, and young adults with this disease because anything is possible with God! My son had a meeting with his therapist the next week and he wasn't in good spirits that day at all. We hadn't been to church in two weeks which didn't help the matter, because when we go, it helps our week go better, so the meeting was due for Xman and his therapist.

The therapist had 45 minutes with Xman. He talked about school, home, and just life in general, what happened in his day, and what sets off triggers and so on. Sometimes after the meeting the therapist will ask me, or I'll ask him how it went; he'll give me a little insight on the conversation they had. One particular time, my son was very upset and depressed, he even wrote a poem to express how he was feeling of which I read later that made me very sad and concerned about the way he was feeling. It went like this; it was titled My Sad Poem... There is always sadness in my heart every day, the pain won't even go away. It feels like I'm a burden to everything I do, the depression inside me I will never lose. This is why my life sucks for me and haunts me every time, that's why I read my sad poem so that I can cry, then the people will understand why that I'm nothing inside.

Xman had shared that with his therapist and the therapist gave it to me so that I could read it. It broke me down; I got so worried about if he could be contemplating suicide or what? As a parent I was confused, hurt for my baby, even though he's a teen, he's still and always will be my baby. I couldn't sleep. I didn't want to say the wrong thing. All I could do was pray and ask the Lord to intervene in this horror. Today wasn't a good morning at all, my son woke up, and he didn't like the way his hair looked, so I told him I would help him fix it, he started throwing a tantrum. He threw things, one of his hair products went everywhere, he hit me real hard on my arm. I got worried that he might do something even worse so, I called the prayer line and they prayed with me and asked for that rebellious spirit to leave him, before I knew it, his father showed up and talked to him, the prayer

911, Broken. **Give it to God!**

was answered, Xman settled down. Even before his dad came, Xman started talking different to me, just as if a whole different feeling in him kicked in. So, I know from experience that prayer works. I prayed for him to have a great day, after all, he is my son and I do love him, and I don't want anything to happen to him.

CHAPTER 3:

I.E.P. Meetings & Tantrums

New day, 9/21/2018, yesterday my child, well rather teen son, had an I.E.P. meeting (Individual Education Program) which tells you what to expect in goals for your child's curriculum and where he should be and when, to be able to keep up. So, I go to the school to find the room we're supposed to meet in, most of the teachers and staff members came. I wanted all his academic teachers there but only one showed up, his English teacher. Xman's grades have been dropping because of either low-test scores or missing assignments, now I was told that he was to have a good support team working with him, but not so. They dropped the ball like last year and it seemed like Xman had just given up due to the problems of last year. I saw a class that he was failing in, and I told his counselor who was there, to change that class to a modified class. He's a junior in high school now, and next year a senior. I had to do what was best for him so that he could keep up. They never told me that almost all his classes had been modified until the end of last year. I should have been told ahead of time, that's why he couldn't keep up in general education classes. Once you modify, it's hard to go back to a general education class, it gets too hard, and more stressful to keep up. My son was an A/B student and had mostly General Education classes before. He had worked so hard, and he made it to generalized education meaning, a regular class setting with kids in the general population, I was very upset. This also frustrates him dearly. My son had a tantrum the other day so bad that he punched a hole through my living room wall, and we have many other holes all through the house from previous episodes. Tomorrow, he goes to therapy, they suggested that he see a psychiatrist, but we haven't yet, because I know they're going to want to put him on medication. I'm eventually going to take him to see one, maybe they can get down to the root of the problem, but until then, I'll keep him in prayer, because it could be worse, like not being able to talk and walk, he could be rocking back and forth or spitting, hitting and so forth. I thank the Lord for as far as Xman has come.

This weekend was pretty good. I finally got in contact with Xman's father, and asked him to take Xman to church, and he said OK. Now normally, it's like pulling hens teeth to get him to go, Xman's dad was going faithfully at one time but just stopped. I'm not counting, because I miss church sometimes too. I can't call the kettle black, but I do think his lifestyle has changed drastically. However, he took Xman to church, gotta give him credit for that! Now don't get me wrong, my lifestyle had also taken a turn for the worse with all these fights, worrying, sprinkled with a lot of stress with my son, and other issues. I got back into some of my old habits, and I need to own it.

From experience, I know for a fact that everyone needs Christ, we've all come up short sometimes, God is very important when you're dealing with this world, because you run across a lot of demons in it, issues that are hard to resolve on your own, the Lord gave us a Comforter, the Holy Spirit that can direct our steps. I have to remind myself of that help from the Holy Spirit. How do you get the Holy Spirit? You have to be saved, read how in the Bible, Romans 10:9.

Right now, I'm doing a lot better than I was, I take things one day at a time. I'm just talking about today L.O.L. God's not through with me, I went to church, and they had this guy that was a speaker from another one of our churches there that day. This guy I'll never forget, I had seen him before giving a testimony, he was very funny, he happened to be at this service in one of our other churches at a different location, I was shocked to see him at this location, I hadn't been to church in almost a month, and it was time to go back. I could feel it in my spirit, something pushing me, telling me I needed to go. I stayed in all weekend, no company, didn't go anywhere, no drinking, and I made it to church. This guy was on fire, I couldn't stop crying,

I.E.P. Meetings & Tantrums

the music was great, no distractions. The message was about worry, and fear, (the condition of being afraid) Philippians 4:12-13 and 2 Timothy 1:7. He gave more than that but that's just a taste of what he was talking about. I could so relate to him. I really enjoyed the service. After church was over, he invited anyone that hadn't and wanted to receive Christ, another guy came out, and dismissed everyone. When I turned around the speaker (the guy that was funny) was right behind me, staring at me in my face. I immediately gave him a big hug, and he told me that he had a word for me. I said, "out of all these people, why me"? He said God told him to tell me everything is going to be alright, and it's my time now. I ran with it, and cried the whole way home. I needed that word so bad; I was feeling empty and asking myself what's next! I was tired, and to show you how the Lord works, on the way home I saw my son and his father, his dad honked the horn at me when I was on the same street but going in the opposite direction, they were on their way to church... Amen. Now everything seemed to be going just fine for a while, then my son lost his key to the house, he thought that someone took it. There was another big blow up about it, it got so bad that I had to play like I was calling the police, he started to beg me not to. I then called his fathe,r and he said that he would come and talk to Xman but he never showed up. The next morning, we went through it again. This time it was about going to school, he didn't want to go, it was hard to get him out the door, he almost missed the bus.

I know the neighbors heard us yelling outside, I was so embarrassed, I just wanted to hide under a rock and disappear if possible. Xman's therapy meeting is coming up and I'm so happy, I pray that it helps. I'm going to let the therapist know all about the blow up and just to let you know, he found the key under his bed, how about that. The day he lost the key, he threw everything on his dresser off and when he got home from school, he wanted me to put all his stuff that he threw back for him. I told him "You threw it off, so you do it yourself". We hadn't made it to church that Sunday so here comes the beginning of the next week. Monday good, Tuesday OK, Wednesday, a little flare up, Thursday a little flare up, Friday a Hot Mess. Xman didn't want to leave on time. It was like hell trying to get him out the door to go to school. He started complaining as we approached his bus stop, he said his head hurt so I rushed him home and got some aspirin. As we went into the house to get the aspirin, I remembered that I didn't take all my keys. I had unattached the ignition key from the house keys and proceeded to the door of the house, got the aspirin. I gave my son a glass of water with the aspirin, he took it. Now we are running on the late side, I didn't want him to miss the bus so we left the house to get in the car, wouldn't you know it, I couldn't find my car key that I left in the ignition. I was a mess. I was looking on the ground, I was sweating, my hair everywhere, I looked between the seats, and in the back of the car. I finally went back in the house, and I broke down crying. I knew we had missed the bus. I was exhausted, and now I had a headache. My son then tells me he wants to stay home because he's not feeling well. About 20 minutes later, I started looking for the keys again, and I found them on the side of the driver seat down at the very bottom in between the seat, and the console in the middle of the car. I remembered the day before which was Thursday, my son telling me that two guys at school were calling him names like retard, and gay. It hurt me to my heart. I was so upset I could have cried right then and there; I know now that's the reason why he didn't want to go to school that day, he could have dropped my keys down in the bottom of the car also.

My heart and my soul were so heavy, I went to bed in tears that night, the next morning I still felt the same way. That's why I know the devil started to attack me, because he knew I was at my lowest, I had lost my keys, that alone threw me for a loop. My son said he had a headache when he probably didn't, he just didn't want to see those guys that were teasing him at school. He was bullied for the 100th time. That Friday he had a therapy session with his doctor that he sees for behavior management due to blowups, and tantrums. I spoke with the therapist, Dr. N. we'll call him, he told me at the appointment Xman had about a week ago, that my son was still in the depression zone but he's talking a lot more on his own. He also said Xman spoke about being a burden to the teachers, and that he was masking anger towards the teachers. He said my son feels that the teachers aren't really interested in helping the students with challenges, and that the majority of them are there just for a paycheck.

The doctor also said they did give Xman a depression assessment test, and he is still depressed like I said earlier, not as bad as before, but still. To top it off, the next weekend our dog ran off overnight, and we couldn't find her. I went from house to house in our neighborhood after I had dropped Xman off at his bus stop. My son was so hurt because we thought the dog would have been back by the morning, she does go around the corner sometimes to play with the other dogs. Mostly everyone in my neighborhood knows her and what she looks like. I asked several people on each block, a couple of people said they saw a black and white Husky, but our dog is a Border Collie, black and white. When my son got to the bus stop and got out of the car, he slammed the door so hard that morning that, I thought he had broken my car window. I knew this would be a trigger for him to flare up.

I started checking with different facilities like the SPCA and the Animal Humane Center, but nothing, no Zoe, that's our dog's name. I was so overwhelmed I couldn't stop riding around in the area, occasionally stopping, and leaving my phone number, and description of my dog. We've lived here for about a year or so, I didn't know everyone, but I've met some in passing and the people I did meet were super nice. I called Xman's dad, and he said that he also went by the SPCA, I told him I had been there too, and the Animal Humane Center as well as looking all over the neighborhood. I remembered that the guy at the Humane Center asked if our dog was chipped and she was. When I adopted her the adoption place microchipped all of the pets that come in there, so I found my file on Zoe, and sure enough there was her chip number.

I called and reported to them that my dog was lost, they told me what they do if she's found by someone and turned into one of the shelters, or, if the shelter picks her up, she will be scanned, and her information will allow them to contact me. That's only if she's turned in. If someone just wants to keep her, because they found her on the street, there's no way to find her. My son phoned me later that day from school and told me that he wants his dog back today. I told him to pray on it, because I haven't found her yet.

He was so upset he started to cry, he also said he's been stabbing himself with pencils. I was beside myself, and about to fall apart. I was trying to stay strong; it was more than enough. I got off the phone, and called the prayer line. About 30-45 minutes later, a guy from down the street that I had told my dog was missing, along with another guy in a red truck knocked at my door, the guy in the red truck told me that Zoe, our dog, was at his house with his daughter. God answers prayer! I grabbed the guy, hugged him and told him "God bless you". He then told me he would have his daughter come outside, and bring Zoe out. He lived just two blocks down from my house around the corner. I followed him to his house and there was Zoe, I started crying, silly me. My dog was happy, and running back and forth. I told the little girl that if she wanted, she could dog sit sometimes, and I would pay her if I had to go out of town or something. I could see it in her eyes that she really got attached to Zoe. I praise God for Zoe's return, looked like things were starting to look up, and calming down.

Now, it's time to pick up Xman from school. When I got there, I found out from him that he was being bullied, I had remembered that not too long ago he had been acting different when I've come to pick him up and his demeanor had changed, he wasn't talking, just looking down, he seemed very depressed, sad looking. He told me he didn't want to go back to school. The following Monday he said he didn't feel well, and wanted to stay home. I said yes, I knew in my heart that it was about the bullying. The next step I thought to myself, was to get to the bottom of this and don't procrastinate, so, I called the principal and set up an appointment for an emergency meeting. I told him to have the two developmental skills teachers along with himself in the meeting. We had the meeting. I let him know what Xman said about the bullying. My son didn't want to give us any names. His teacher said that Xman had been going to school counseling and he had told the counselor the name of the bully. The principal said that he would ask the counselor about it and pull the bully out of class, and have him come to his office. The bully had been calling my son retarded in front of his peers, and no telling what else. Over the past weekend Xman stayed isolated in his room.

CHAPTER 4:

Triggers

This wasn't the only bullying he experienced, one time a girl that Xman knew poured milk on him at lunch time in front of people as my son was eating, another time a guy that was in one of my son's classes stole his phone out of his classroom and just so happened one of the aides overheard some kids talking about where the guy hid it, she got it back. One other time that I knew about was when this guy at school took my son's expensive Beats earphones, the list goes on... I don't know all of it, because my son doesn't want me to know really, he tries to hold it all in. I told the principal to make stiffer consequences for these perpetrators, and send a message to their parents, never happened. This is so crucial for these kids with the challenge of Autism, it's frustrating, humiliating. It affects their grades, the schools are supposed to have zero tolerance for bullying and it's hard for them to bounce back, and then it spills over into the home. These are triggers.

I haven't heard back from the principal or anything about it from his teachers. I don't know if you remember, but I mentioned earlier that I had been seeking legal help. I sent this information about all the mishaps, the bullying, and the algebra teacher to my attorney, because I went ahead with the case. I also called the principal back again, because he never called me back, nor have any of his teachers. I have asked his teacher to call me, and it's been over a week, and no call back, and left several messages for the principal, now I'm having problems with his new math teacher that is not changing my son's grades on time when he hands in his work assignments, the principal said he would handle the problem the day after I told him about the counselor who knew the bully's name. When I spoke to the office manager, she made up all kinds of excuses why the principal hadn't returned my calls, and I told her that I need a call back today or I'll probably publicize this to the news. This is very serious, and the school brags about zero bullying tolerance, "Great Job!"

Finally, the principal called back, he just said he talked to Xman about the bullying, he said my son told him it only happened once and that my son said he just let it go. I really questioned this, you have to remember the principal never came through for us the day he said he was going to find out the name or names of the bullies, and is just now calling back, almost a week and a half later. I had also told the principal about all the incidents that occurred prior to this, and this wasn't the first time. The principal asked me was it this year, I told him this incident was this year, but what difference did it make if you're still at the same school, and if you have a zero-tolerance policy for bullying here at this school, for your information, it happened last year several times. This really needs to be reiterated to the parents, and kids. There needs to be stiffer consequences, kids have killed themselves behind bullying. It's no joke when you find out about it, it needs to be addressed immediately. Like I said before, these are signs and triggers.

Thanksgiving holiday was coming up, and grades. My son's grades had dropped due to all this drama. I'm not surprised, here we go. I requested another emergency I.E.P. meeting (an Individual Education Program meeting). I got a call from the vice principal stating that we would set up a date soon as they got back from the holiday. They're back to school now and I haven't heard anything since they've been back. My son and I needed that break to get out of town and see some of the family, my mother, daughter, my brother, and some friends. However, we didn't get a chance to see my dad, he's been in the process of moving to another state. I know how that can be, I'll see him, and his wife soon. I brought my son down there, because the family also wanted to talk with Xman about his behavior, outbursts and tantrums, it was out of hand. They have been worried about me. They think he might hurt me if he gets mad enough on accident. Thank God we have an appointment coming up soon with his therapist and now, I'm making his appointments a month in advance.

I started making four appointments in advance, this increases his help, and he gets to be seen more often, like possibly three to four times a month for therapy. They're back to school now from the holiday, and this is the end of the first week. I asked Xman about his classes and how he was doing in his academics, especially Science and English. I know these are his favorite classes, and he gets good grades in them, he just gestured by shrugging his shoulders. He also said they had an assignment in English class, and it was about Salem, and witches doing witchcraft naked. He said his teacher started reading them a story about it then showed them a video of the characters naked doing witchcraft. I was so upset I almost blew it! First, on something like this, they should get consent from the parents. Second, what does this have to do with English? It's perverted, it also plants a seed in the innocent mind. I immediately called my attorney's office, and they told me to document it. That was very unacceptable. I will be mentioning this in his I.E.P. meeting coming up. I got sick over the weekend, the I.E.P. was the week I was sick.

I called the school to speak with one of Xman's teachers in Special Needs class which is called Developmental Skills class, and I got one of his teachers Mr. M. I asked him for Xman's grades from the last report card and Mr. M. said he would call me back in 5 minutes, I waited about 20 minutes, no call. I called back and the other teacher answered, I asked him the same thing, what were Xman's last grades, and he gave them to me. There were two grades that I was very concerned about, as I said before, and that was his Science which he got a C in, unacceptable, he usually gets and A or B+, and that was when he was in some General Education classes without being modified. The other class was Modern History, and his grade dropped from a B to a D- in Mrs. S.'s class, and I asked why did his grade drop? Mr. M. in his skills class said he didn't want to take his final, and Mr. M. said that Xman told him that I said he didn't have to take the final, I told Mr. M. that I never said that, and why didn't anyone bring it to my attention. Then, Mr. M. changed his story, and said the grade dropped because he took the final and got a low grade, so now I don't know what to believe due to Mr. M. changing his story. I also called the vice principal, Mr. V., to schedule an I.E.P. meeting, waiting on a call back. That was about a week ago, and still, no call back yet. I already left one message, then I made a second call. I finally spoke to his assistant, Ms. J., and left another message. I called back later that afternoon, spoke to Ms. J. and she said Mr. V. was in another meeting. I told Ms. J. that I would be calling Special Education, then she says, "you don't want to wait?", I told her "I've waited long enough", why should I? About 30 minutes later he calls me back, Mr. V., the vice principal, finally. I told him I need to get our date for the I.E.P. meeting so I'll know what I'm doing because I also have other engagements myself. Mr. V. says that he would get right back to me, he called back, I had already given him three dates that would work so we finally made the date. If I wouldn't have called Special Education, I believe he would have avoided me for as long as he could.

I spoke to the vice principal, Mr. V. the week of Christmas Vacation and told him that I would be in contact with him when they got back to school and make the I.E.P. appointment around the first or second week, as soon as they returned from their vacation. The end of the week before Christmas Vacation, my son told me he had a meeting with his therapist that Friday, and I was so glad that was the last day of school before vacation, he needed that meeting because he started talking more about depression coming on and how he hates his life again. I took him to see the doctor and he had told me the meeting went well, my son opened up, and got a lot out. When that happens, it's better for the both of us. He gets to vent and gets whatever is in him out. Now it's Christmas Vacation and I'm so happy, we don't have to get up early, we're not going out of town or anything, but we can do whatever we want locally. I had a lot of shopping, and mailing and gift wrapping to do. My son and I, and his dad met to pick up the Christmas tree, and Xman was very excited about that. My son decorated it, and it came out really nice. I always used to use my mom's ornaments, they were so pretty, my mother had a lot of style. During his vacation he asked if he could catch the bus to the mall by himself, I told him yes, so he took the bus that he catches to go to school, that took him all the way to the mall. Before he left the house, he

Triggers

was very nervous. I just reassured him that it's just like going to school, and you don't even have to transfer, just one bus. I gave him the names of the streets he was to get off on. I told him that he'd see the Mall anyway, and he could get off where he wanted. He felt a lot better, so his dad came over, and gave him some money and dropped him off at the bus stop. My son always keeps a phone on him, or he can't go anywhere, those are the rules. He got to the mall, and I called him, it happened to be when he arrived. I was so happy and proud he made it; he was also elated with joy.

When he got to the mall, he got himself something to eat and went to his favorite stores. He called me up after a while and told me he ran out of money and was ready to come home. Now here's the kicker, he told me he was confused on how to get back. I explained to him that he would have to cross the street and look for the bus stop. I also told him to take the same bus number back. He had a problem locating a bus stop, and kind of got confused again on where to cross the street. He finally got it and found a stop. He got on the bus, the same number as he caught to get there like I told him, but the bus driver told him that he doesn't go to his destination. So, he got off the bus right away and called me, he was a little frantic. I finally got him to calm down. I called his dad and had him go pick him up, it was starting to get dark. I was even confused when my son told me it was the same number bus, he took down there only, it didn't go all the way back, it didn't make sense to me, well at least he had enough sense to get off the bus before he rode too far.

That was a good thing, I was still very proud of him for even making the effort. Going back to Thanksgiving holiday vacation, we had gone to see my mother, she had had a little stroke in her eye and had to have an operation on it. My mother told me that she wanted us to come, plus I hadn't had a chance to see my grandkids, the two girls, ages six and eight, also other friends and family. We used to live in Southern California where they are, but I moved about eleven to twelve years ago further north. The oldest girl does cheerleading, and the youngest is also very active as well, and has a lot of wisdom beyond her little years. The oldest also loves to swim, and is very good at it, she is head of her cheerleading team. That weekend when we got there, it was my oldest granddaughters cheerleading competition match at UC Irvine in a big auditorium at the college. My brother came with his girlfriend, Xman and I, my daughter and of course the two girls, and my mother. My granddaughter lead it, she was just eight at the time and the youngest in the group. She has a beautiful stage presence, and she pumps up the other cheerleaders. Xman loved every minute of the competition, it kept his attention. We were there for at least four hours, and they had 30-40 groups competing. My granddaughters group won first place for Pasadena, California, and now they'll be performing in Las Vegas, we are all very proud of her.

CHAPTER 5:

More Tantrums

It's back to school time from Christmas Vacation, and wouldn't you know it, the bus route changed. That meant that the bus Xman used to take doesn't go as far and he'll have to transfer to another bus. First day back, he gets lost, he took the wrong bus, he calls me up, I ask him what street he was on, he tells me, and I don't know where that is. I ask him if he's by a store or gas station, and he says no but he wants to walk down to the main street. He tells me the name of the Main Street and I said, "go for it", that's the street he's supposed to be on. Once you get on the Main Street, I had spoken with him again and he told me he saw a bus stop with the number of the right bus, he got on the bus and he's on his way to school. Then, the bus breaks down and he has to get off and walk the rest of the way there. At this point he's very frustrated, he makes it to school a little late. Second day, he catches the first bus and gets it right. Praise the Lord! After that he calls me up, and says he missed the other bus that he transfers to, and could I pick him up and take him the rest of the way to school, I said OK.

I picked him up, and to my surprise, there sits the bus that he's supposed to catch just sitting there on a break waiting for time to leave. I get out of my car and ask the bus driver if he goes to the streets that my son is going to school to, he says "yes". The bus driver said that my son came and asked him that, and just walked away. That was the right bus, now I ask my son why you told me that that was the wrong bus, and that you missed it. My son then told me the bus driver wasn't clear on what he was saying, it sounds like an excuse. I'm trying to give him the benefit of the doubt. When we get in the car from the bus stop, we start arguing, one thing leads to another and my son started banging on my car dashboard, he started fighting me, and I almost had two car wrecks on the way to take him to school. It got so bad that when I approached the school, I had to make him get out and walk the rest of the way. When I got home, I called the prayer line. I was so distraught and hurt that I called his dad, and told him to pick Xman up after school, he told me he couldn't do it that day.

I had explained to his father what had happened, and he told me he would pick him up the next day, because he was getting his car fixed and it would be finished. I really needed help that day, I had also said something to my son that I shouldn't have out of anger. I felt really bad, and I was very sorry. At noon that day, I received a phone call from my son, he said he had also spoke to his father, and he wanted to apologize, and I also apologized to him as well. I then went to pick my son up, and he said he was sorry again. I told him for his actions he would have consequences, so I put up some of his electronics. He asked me when he would be getting them back, and I told him it depended on his behavior. This weekend we went to church, and I had a prayer partner pray for my son and I for peace in the home, and for confidence over my son. Now anytime we have a problem I call the prayer line because I know, over the holidays I stopped smoking and drinking, I know it's all because of prayer. I was spending nine to eleven dollars one to two times a week on cigarettes alone. Some weekends I would try and drown my problems out with drinking, etc... My son started to ask me "mom, are you going to stop smoking and drinking?" I would try to hide it from him, but he knew I had a problem, he wasn't stupid. I'd say "yes", and I'd even say to myself if he only knew how hard I wanted to stop. I was so tired of school, tired of fighting with him, tired of bills, and myself. Then the Lord just said that's enough and took the craving away. Thank you, God! Don't get me wrong, I will never be perfect, we're always going to have trials, and tribulations. I know that the Lord will equip me with whatever I need to get through all this even though sometimes I feel I don't have it all together. That's when I need to tap into God and just ask. Don't ever be afraid to ask. Remember, that when the Lord says you have not because you ask not! He

More Tantrums

reigns! I know that if I didn't believe, I would have never been able to deal with all of this. The Lord is the only thing that saved me from snapping!

I would have either been in jail or dead, and so would my son. This week my son and I fell out again in my car on the way to school today, it was a little rainy, and we started arguing. He started to pound on my dashboard, and I told him several times not to hit on any parts of my car, or me. He told me as I was driving that he hates school and didn't want to go. I asked him if anyone was bothering him, and he said not now. Then I asked him, "did anything happen recently"? He didn't really elaborate on it. Then he told me he just didn't want to go, and his life sucks. I was trying to tell him to stop talking negatively about his life, and himself. I also told him school is for learning and even though he didn't mention that anything was bothering him, I just wanted to let him know, not to worry about trivial matters, to go for the right reasons, to learn and keep up his grades. Don't be bothered with negative people and stay away from drama. I also told him about his foul language, or I'm going to start taking away more of his electronics.

I already had to take away his Dr. Dre music Bluetooth, and Xbox games. Today, he has a meeting with his therapist. I'm so glad, he needs to vent, and sometimes it's better to talk to someone that's a good listener and a professional. We went to the therapist on Friday, on our way, Xman's acting very short tempered and sarcastic, so I asked him how his day was, he told me it wasn't so good, I asked him what happened, and he wouldn't go into detail. I then told him, well, we're on our way to the doctor's office, maybe he can help. Then my son started talking about the therapist and how he's not really helping. When we get there, the therapist comes out and asked me how everything was going. I told him not so good; he then asked me to come back to his office to talk before my son's session. I went back and told the therapist that we had a very bad blow up this week in the car to the point of getting very physical, I then left his office. He called my son in, and I asked him about how long they were going to be today, and he said about 35 minutes. I went home while Xman was in session to start dinner. Now, normally I don't cook on Fridays, because by then I might just be exhausted. Anyway, I did this time. When 35 minutes had passed, I was there back at the doctor's

31

office to pick Xman up. The doctor came out and said they had a good session, on the other hand my son said they didn't, he said the doctor's not helping because he doesn't give him any solutions to his problems. He just tells him that his anger can get him in trouble but, no calming techniques or anything. My son ended up telling me he was bullied again by some bald guy, and someone else earlier that week. I told my son to write everything down, and I will bring all of this up at the I.E.P. meeting coming up. I called the prayer line and prayed about the I.E.P. meeting. That evening my son was trying to open a can of soup and cut his thumb real deep, and he went into a rage, he started throwing glasses, and other glassware insight all over the kitchen and screaming. I was trying to calm him down, he wouldn't listen, I called 911 for an ambulance, and the people could hear him swearing, and screaming in the background.

I couldn't control him at all, 911 sent the police out, two officers came to my house and asked what happened to my son, and I told them that he cut his thumb on the lid of the New England Clam Chowder can. They asked me if I wanted an ambulance to still come out, but Xman didn't want them to take him. I told him that I had a ride coming for him, because I remembered also that the last time, I took the ambulance they tried to charge me close to $1000.00, and they did the same thing to a friend of mine. I had a way for him anyway, his father came and took him to Urgent Care, they put dissolving stitches in him, and disinfected it, and wrapped it up. My kitchen was covered with glass, it was a mess. Xman called me up and called me every name but a child of God. He kept saying I'm going to die, over and over. I forgot to mention that before he left with his father and his father's girlfriend that were picking him up to take him to Urgent Care, he and I came back into the house after the police left, and Xman started breaking more things in the house, I was so nervous, and beside myself. I could feel my heart beating faster, and faster. I was so glad when they finally pulled up to take him and get him out of the house. When he saw them, he knew that he had to act calm. They got him and they left, but I was a wreck.

When he got back from Urgent Care, he was still acting a little cocky. I gave him and myself something for anxiety, a Benadryl, I told him he had

More Tantrums

to take it, or I would call the police again, and so he did, we both went to sleep. The next day, due to Xman's sore throat and thumb incident, he stayed home and didn't go to school for a few days the week of the I.E.P., so, we couldn't have it that week. I had to reschedule it for another time. I did let the school know, I hated to do that. I called and spoke to the vice principal of his school, Mr. V., and we agreed to reschedule, he was supposed to send me the paperwork, and get the date. We had two options of dates open for the I.E.P. meeting, but we had never confirmed them, so I called him back, the vice principal told me that we had already set a date, I told him no we didn't, but what date do you have down? He told me the date, and I told him I never got anything, and never received the documents confirming the date, but that it would be alright with me the day he had chosen. That's just how unorganized they were, trying to make me feel like I was incompetent. I thought to myself, sorry, try something new, because I'm not the one to play with at this point.

If I don't get the paperwork soon, I will have to change the date. The paperwork is proof of the meeting and what it's about, this makes it a record that there was a meeting, and why. You must have it on record, also my son told me yesterday that the algebra teacher, Mr. L., is still up to his old tricks. Still playing loud music in the class while the students are trying to concentrate, and how my son knows is because the music is so loud you can hear it down the corridor of the school. My son also said that a lot of the kids at the school are complaining about Mr. L.'s sarcastic attitude with them and how he criticizes them. I told Xman he needs to get the names of the other students that are having trouble with him, write down what he said to them as a matter of record. I don't understand why they haven't done anything about him yet. He sure isn't a self-esteem builder at all. My son went to his therapy also yesterday, we'll see how that went. I haven't gotten the report from the therapist yet but when I do, I'll document that too.

This weekend there was another blow up with my son because the cable TV was acting up and I had to call a technician at our cable company to come out and fix it. My son started swearing and throwing things again because of it. I had to call his dad to see if he could calm Xman down over the phone, that's if I can catch him because it's very hard to catch up with him. Well, I finally did catch up with him. This time, he talked to our son, and it helped a little, the TV came back on, and everything went well. I told my son; you can't blow up with the people that are trying to help us. You're going to have to understand that this is not the end of the world just because these things happen. We're never going to have a perfect life on earth. There will always be trials and tribulations. After our conversation I went to bed, I told him we need to make it to church this weekend. We made it. I received the I.E.P. meeting letter to confirm the appointment date, but once again, it doesn't tell me why the meeting was called or that this is an emergency I.E.P. meeting. It is very important that it says that so that you can refer to it, so there is no mistake on what the meeting was about so that everyone is in one accord.

CHAPTER 6:

I.E.P. Meetings & Suicide Scares

will be calling today about it and speak with the vice principal. I want it documented like it's supposed to be. Just last week I told the vice principal to please write my concerns down on the I.E.P. so that everyone will know why, and what it's about. He then told me, will do, they're playing with me, and I don't like it. It's unfair, in the name of the Lord, I will get it done right. Yesterday, my son came home wearing a rainbow-colored rubber bracelet what now stands for Gay Rights, they even perverted the rainbow. I asked him where he got it from, he told me that his teacher gave it to him. I don't know about you, but I have rights as a parent to question a lot of what's going on at school as far as curriculum, things that we don't agree with such as, forcing it on the students, such as personal lifestyles, everyone knows that teens are very impressionable. If a teacher has a question, whether it's right or wrong, to do something instead of guessing, consult the parents, because I was upset about it. Plus, that same teacher speaks about her home life, and how her, and her wife are raising their children etc... That's not what my child is going to school to learn, especially, not about her life, but to get his basic education. Just spoke to the Vice Principal today, he says will have the Developmental Skills teacher phone me and put the info into the I.E.P. that concerns me on my son's behalf. I also told the V.P. about the rainbow bracelet. The same teacher showed a movie of Salem where witchcraft goes on, and the people were running around naked. What is wrong with their mind I'm wondering to myself. These were my concerns, and I wanted all this info entered, and documented on the paperwork of the I.E.P. meeting.

(1) Parental consent on questionable material done in class, and if not ok with parent, to give something equivalent in grading, like another project. (2) Prompting Xman to hand in work on time so he won't fall behind. (3) If he falls behind in any assignment to please give him notice to get caught up so that it won't affect his grades. (4) To give notice to parent of any distractions, bullying, etc... so, it can quickly be resolved so, it won't affect his grades. I think this is more than fair, and the right thing to do.

I also called the lady in charge of my son's school at Special Ed Headquarters in our city and left a message to call me back regarding the I.E.P. meeting. I was wondering why my son had had an attitude for the past few weeks, and that Saturday before we went to church, he had told me that he hates everything, people, school, and asked me, why do bad things happen to good people? I tried to tell him to stop talking so negatively, and that there will be good days and bad days, trials and tribulations for everyone on earth, not until you make it to heaven will everything go great. He told me that all he wants to do is just live like a hermit and isolate. He left my room where we were talking, and I got so depressed, the devil started working on me as soon as he said that. I started to cry when I heard this. I hated to hear that my only son, that I loved so much, felt like this, and I can only pray that he comes out of this depression, and this way of thinking toward the world. He also told me since he was in elementary school he's been mistreated. He also told me about quite a few episodes that happened to him, and that now he tells me when he takes up for himself, he's the one that gets in trouble. How do you think as a parent that makes you feel to know that this is the way my son sees life through his eyes, no hope.

We finally had the I.E.P. meeting and I spoke to everyone, and we all seemed to be on the same page except, for his English teacher that I had mentioned, into the witchcraft, that got up and left, without acknowledging why, and what she did these things for. All the other teachers in his academics said they would be working with Xman and have their aides on top of everything to see that he gets his work in on time and see that his grades don't drop. Even his science teacher said he would give up his lunch to help him keep up. His history teacher told me Xman's grade will be going up.

I.E.P. Meetings & Suicide Scares

So, everything seems to start looking up. The V.P. told me he would see to it that the bullying would stop, and he found out the same guy was doing the bullying all this time, but there had been other incidences between now and last year that I spoke of earlier. Two weeks later, Xman was called into the office regarding a letter that he himself wrote out of frustration because of the bullying, and he went to the counselor at the school to talk because he was having a bad day.

First, I spoke to Mr. M. in his Developmental Skills class about his new report card, and he told me that Xman's grades had dropped again. Now remember, we just had an I.E.P. meeting, and everyone signed in agreement to it, as far as prompting him and keeping him on track. I guess they all of a sudden, forgot what they said at the I.E.P meeting, that his grades were going up, and everything will be just great. If this were so, then why are the grades going down. I was beside myself once again. I spoke to the Vice Principal Mr. V. about it, and he didn't sound very concerned at all. This is the same man that told me my child had been working very hard in class and all these distractions with bullying and interrogating him without getting me, the parent involved or permission first. My son said he felt dehumanized, the police were there, the V.P., Mr. V., and another lady that spoke with him without my knowledge. He missed 2 periods of class behind it, for a child with Autism this was very frightening and intimidating to say the least. All behind a letter that he wrote when he was being bullied and talking about it to one of his counselors to vent, when I had told them previously that Xman had his own Therapist, and I didn't consent or sign any consent papers to speak to anyone on the school grounds. As a parent, to know what my child is learning and watching, especially something that serious and wicked, I'm speaking about the witchcraft, interrogation, and so on, it's imperative. I was very upset about all of it and my child told me it bothered him as well, it was too much, this was on Friday, right before we both got sick, when he told me how he felt about all this stuff.

Now, the last day of school before the Christmas holiday break my son started talking about being depressed, he did have an appointment with his therapist. Then during his break, this was around December 17th through

911, Broken. **Give it to God!**

January 7, 2019, one day on his break he started talking about suicide again and we weren't going to have another meeting with his therapist until January 18th, this was getting very crucial. These dates I put down were very important, because like I mentioned earlier in the book, I had been filing legal action due to all of this, so periodically you might hear me mention dates, because I was documenting a lot to have it as a matter of record.

I spoke to my son Xman again about the incident when he was called into the office for questions, and about the letter he wrote about the bullying, and Xman told me that he didn't show it to anyone. Xman just said that he had been having a bad day that day, and he went to see a counselor by the name of Mrs. F. He told the counselor that he writes his feeing down on paper. Then the counselor called the office and had him summoned to the office, they then told him he had to speak with the Vice Principal Mr. V.,

they also called the police and another lady Mrs. L. in to interrogate him. He missed two of his class periods. They went through his backpack, his phone, read all his private stuff. I was never called until after the matter. My son said, like I said earlier, he felt dehumanized, he said they were looking down on him. They didn't try to talk to resolve anything, it was simply harassment. Mrs. L., the unknown lady there, said he should be thrown out of school because he's a threat. To me, it was a setup, due to the I.E.P meeting because of what my concerns were with my son. They were taking it out on him and trying to intimidate him. So, what the Vice Principal said about trying to help him was all a lie. My son had also told me he told the counselor when he writes stuff on paper it calms him down, but she used that as a way to set him up. She knew his condition with Autism and tried to use his handicap against him. To me it was all plotted and premeditated. This was very cruel and disturbing. I just don't know who to trust anymore. You would think that the people they hire in our school system would have more compassion. This all affected my son's grades as well as humiliated a child with a disability. He was in fear, he feels he can't trust anyone, and his self-esteem is low due to this treatment. Then, this is when the twist went down, when he went to see that counselor, it was time for report cards to come out, remember, I had first spoken to his Development Skills teacher

I.E.P. Meetings & Suicide Scares

about his report card. The Skills teacher told me his grades and they had dropped, some of them, and the others had stayed the same, so they didn't change at all, and the grades that were supposed to go up never changed either. I was very upset.

After all this, I ended up in the E.R. at the Hospital twice due to abdominal cramps and shortness of breath, this is called Diverticulitis, that's the medical term for stomach cramps, and I get it every time I'm stressed out. The doctors say they still don't know exactly what causes it, but I know after I get very upset it comes on. The second time I went to the E.R. was for shortness of breath, the doctor told me that my lungs weren't clear, and he gave me a very strong steroid, Prednisone 50 mg of it a day, an inhaler, and some sedatives to make me relax. You think I wasn't tired to say the least. I also had to take a CAT Scan for the Diverticulitis to make sure that's what it was. Then they gave me two different antibiotics plus pain killers. I was in excruciating pain due to all of this. I also was put on bed rest. I couldn't get upset about nada or it would flare up again. At this particular time, my son was going through it too. That meant that his attitude was changing and getting frustrated with it all.

He and I were at the end of our rope. The only thing that kept us strong was going to church and reading God's Word to calm us. This Sunday we didn't make it to church but the Sunday before this was Resurrection Day, what the world calls Easter Sunday, and we did go with one of my friends and her mother who also came and it was so good and we had a great week, hadn't started out so good that Monday because my son had a terrible day, and I know why, because the devil will always try to attack when you do what God wants you to do, and that was make it to church. Xman was testing that week in school because it's getting towards the end of the school year, he's a Junior now. We really didn't need any distractions, especially now. He needs to be straight focused on what he's learned so his testing scores stay high. Yesterday, Monday, I noticed he had a pretty bad attitude when he got in the car. He started talking real negative and about suicide, also about some girl at school that's passing around a rumor, telling his other peers that my son is spreading their business around, and telling personal stuff about them as well. I know my son and he's very private about everything. You almost have to pry info out of him. He's not the type to freely open up, so, all of this is a lie. Now, all of his so-called friends, peers, what have you, are not speaking to him because of it. The only way I found out was through my mother because he spoke with her and explained to her what happened, because I couldn't get it out of him. Now he will talk to his grandmother about certain things. I told him I need to call the school, and he told me not to tell them. I also found out that he was invited to Prom by a senior girl, but he never told me nothing about it.

I'm at a standstill. I know prayer works so when I got this news, I called the prayer line and explained to them what was going on and we prayed for my son and these issues. I know if two or more agree touching anything, it will be done on earth as it is in Heaven. Matthew 18:19 Now Xman woke up and told me he didn't sleep all night due to this. He's now unable to make it to school today. I told him he could stay home. After a while he started to talk about what happened and he did tell me the girls' name who was passing around the vicious rumors, then he got upset. I guess I was asking him too many questions, and he started to hit the walls down our home hallways. He put two holes in the wall, also he got mad because I took away his music box. I told him if he stays home, he can either study or watch some T.V. but no music at all. He had told me he was up all night, so that should mean you're tired, so lay down, get some rest, I told him. It's not a party time, plus, he missed taking his test.

I was so upset about the wall we got into an argument; he started talking about taking his life again. We both pushed each other's buttons. You would think because I'm the adult I would be able to hold in my feelings, but you have to remember, enough pressure can break a steel pipe, and not one is perfect. I had to call the suicide hotline for him and his doctor, the Psychologist Dr. N. to get more numbers just in case the one's I had didn't work. At that moment I needed all the help I could get, I needed Jesus! I also called the prayer line again. I needed prayer desperately. This was a disaster gone bad. He finally went in his room. I got him to take some medication and I took some as well, he didn't give me any problems this time about taking them.

I.E.P. Meetings & Suicide Scares

That's how prayer works, matter of fact, we laid down. I had to get some fresh air, so I left and got some of the things I needed to fix the holes in the walls. He got up later and came in to apologize. I also apologized for some of the things I said while upset and hurt too. He told me he would fix the walls and he started right then. I started making calls to all the people I felt that needed to know about this blow-up, due to all the things going on at school and what it does to our home life.

I left a message first for the principal, then Special Ed and Developmental Skills teachers. I got in touch with one of his teachers in Developmental Skills class and told him, Mr. M., that my son wouldn't be coming in today, I also told him why. I told Mr. M. to send a memo to the principal and anyone else who needed to know. I waited for call backs. The Special Ed lady that represents my son's high school called back. I told her everything. I also told her this has been an ongoing problem that hasn't really been addressed properly even after the I.E.P. meeting. Nothing has been done, it's also getting worse. I told her I have a letter from my son's therapist and a note of what happened this time that I'll be sending her, and the therapist was sending the same info to the other people, such as, the Principal, etc. that we felt should know about this crucial situation that hasn't been dealt with. I finally spoke to the Principal and told him what was going on when he returned my call later that day, and how important it is to address this right away because it's effecting my son's mandatory test that he's supposed to take. He'd already missed one day of testing due to the shenanigans. The Principal then told me to send my son to his office the next day and he would nip all this in the bud, and said that Xman would also be able to make up the test he missed. The next day he went to school, and later, I picked him up that afternoon, but he was still moody. I asked him how was his day, and he didn't have much to say. We had a little argument about his teachers that he said asked him questions about some work he had already handed in, that's what got him upset. He told me he didn't want to go back to school again. I told him he only had about a month and a half left until the semester was over, then his summer vacation. This same day he had an appointment with his therapist Dr. N., we had a debate about that too, because he didn't want to see him

911, Broken. **Give it to God!**

again either. Xman told me he wasn't going to the doctors at all, so we went home. His appointment wasn't for another hour, he came into the house still upset. I told him to stop swearing and being so disrespectful to me, and then he threw my phone. We both got on our phones to call his dad, and he went into his room to talk to his father. I also told him how he was acting in my conversation with his dad so, his dad tried to calm him down over the phone. I then asked Xman did he want to go see his therapist, and to my surprise he said yes. I took him to therapy; this was good because he had so much to vent about, and it was a pretty long session. I spoke to the therapist Dr. N. before he went in and read him the letter I wrote to Special Ed, the Principal, and Development Skills class. The letter about the whole situation he was having at school. Then the therapist had a heads up.

I had to seek Legal Help, so, I got an attorney last year because of all of this. It just isn't fair to any child to have to go through this treatment. I also started reading the Book of Proverbs in the Bible to seek wisdom, knowledge and understanding on what to do at this point. I needed justice for my son, and others that are facing the same battle of abuse. In America at this time, the most recent statistics say there's been over 234 shootings at schools, 144 killed not including college, and the average age of the shooters are 18 years and younger. Just speaking about the attorneys, the other day my attorney calls me up and says she's dropping my son's case, because of no physical abuse. I told her how unfair this was and told her, "I guess mental abuse carries no weight, to the point of my child wanting to commit suicide?". So, I guess you have to go ahead and kill yourself then that would be physical! Also, constant bullying how not one, but groups of kids are bullying him, making racial slurs, calling him names as he walks down the school corridors, on campus and around the school. Just yesterday my son was bullied again by the same guy, and one of the guys' friends that I reported to the school about a month ago at the I.E.P. meeting when the vice principal Mr. V., told me he would take care of this. He never did. Just like this attorney, they don't care until It's too late. Then everyone is looking stupid when a bullied victim snaps, when nobody would listen to their cry for help. That could cost innocent children their lives, and parents their grief. No one

I.E.P. Meetings & Suicide Scares

wants that, but yet, several kids are crying out and giving signs of abuse daily, but no one is paying attention.

CHAPTER 7:

Attorney Drops the Ball & 911

My attorney waited a whole year, and then dropped the ball. I was so upset because all my hard work of documenting everything was wasted. Then, she called me back, the attorney says she might have another attorney to handle the case. Mind you, I have a Statute of Limitations were on that, I don't want to run out, at the same time, I'm scrambling around trying to find another attorney. Then my old attorney calls me up again, says Quote-on-Quote, "tell me briefly what happened again and why you're suing". She acted as though she didn't even know what was really going on at all. I was in shock to say the least. That lead me to believe that she hadn't been taking the case seriously at all. The attorney also wanted me to explain while another person was listening to me on the speaker phone. Then she says, "I'll call you back". The attorney finally calls back and says another attorney will be calling you in a few. I was waiting, no call. Then my attorney calls back and says, "I don't have anyone for you so, I'll fax you a form to sign, and fax back to my office, taking me off the case, and I'll file the papers in your name representing your son, and when you find another attorney, then you can sign them on the case to represent your son". I was so hurt, I had been communicating with her paralegal all this time for a whole year and no results, just drops me.

Later on that day, a counselor Mrs. D., phoned from my son's school regarding the letter my son's therapist wrote in reference to the bullying. The letter implied that nothing has been done about it, and that they clearly don't have an understanding of the permanent effects and damage this will have upon a child. I say only God can remove this damage. The therapist Dr. N. also mentioned Xman's depression, and diagnosis with Autism, and other issues it has created. You would think that the Principal or V.P. would of called back, but no, the counselor did instead. I told the school in our I.E.P. meeting that he has his own therapist, and I don't consent to him speaking to anyone else about his personal issues because they seem to twist the stories. Just like last time my son said he wrote how he feels down on paper and told one of the other counselors on the school grounds, and she couldn't wait to make trouble for him, because of her, they called him into the office, kept him for 2 periods, and interrogated Xman with the police officer.

The V.P. and some other lady went through all his belongings, his backpack and his cell phone like he was a convict. They didn't tell me until afterwards. I don't want him talking to any of their office staff, we can't trust them. Then the school counselor still had the audacity to ask me to get a consent from Xman's therapist to release his file to the school. I knew right away this was a set up. I told her this will never happen and to forward that letter from Xman's therapist to the Principal and V.P., she told me "will do". I had already left a message for the Principal to call back, and he never did. That same counselor did tell me she thought my son was very respectable, and how she liked him, and if he needed anything done to help, to get in touch with her. I told her what they need to do is make stiffer bullying rules, also to call in the two boys, and that one girl that has been causing these problems for my son into the office. Those are the ones who need to be questioned like my son was. My son told me it got so bad that a group of kids started taunting him, calling names, making racial slurs, and swearing at him on campus in front of everyone. How would you feel if that was your child, and nothing was done. A Vice Principal called back finally, one I never spoke to before, Mr. S. I told him everything and he said he would handle it, now, you know what I was thinking, I've heard this before.

The last few days have been pretty quiet. The week before this my son went on a suicide rampage and I had to call my son's therapist, 911, for help. He gave me the number for the Suicide Hotline. My son was also grabbing knives to cut himself with. I was trying to stop him but he's so much bigger,

Attorney Drops the Ball & 911

and stronger that it was hard. I fought hard to keep him from cutting himself, and he stopped. The therapist called the police, and the police called me, and I cancelled them because I got scared thinking they might hurt my son. Like I said before, after the V.P. called back, things had settled for a minute that week. Then another episode happened over the weekend, Xman got angry and put 2 holes in my wall and started to talk about suicide again. We were inside the house, and he also pushed me and hit me in my arm very hard. I tried to calm him down, but he wouldn't listen to me. He started slamming doors and knocking over stuff. I called 911, I was afraid of what could happen next to me or to him if I didn't get someone there right away. I just prayed that they sent the right officers, that wouldn't hurt him, but help him, and talk him down. This needed to deescalate, and to let him know there are consequences for his actions. My prayers were answered, they were police that the Lord ordered, very helpful. They called my son outside, made him sit down and listen, and allowed him to vent. They were concerned about his condition and kept all of that in mind. When they were done, they asked me what I wanted them to do. I told them to please reiterate the consequences to Xman, and they did. The police left their card in case I needed them again. I was grateful, thank you Lord!

The end of the next week was Memorial Day holiday, and I was grateful because we had that next Monday off, so we didn't have to get up early. That Friday before the holiday my son got up and said he didn't want to go to school. I told him he only had that Friday to finish, and then, he had a three-day weekend coming up. He didn't care, we argued until I was exhausted. I ended up telling him he could stay home. I didn't want to have to call 911 again so, I just let him stay home to keep the peace. I've been speaking with other attorneys regarding his case against the school district, since the last attorney dropped the ball on me, but she did file in Superior Court, and also made the service, and put the case in my name on my son's behalf. All I need to do now is try to find an attorney to attach to the case. I've been praying about it, it's all in God's hands now. However, that holiday weekend turned out alright. At first, my son's father had told him he would take him to a concert out of town, but he didn't have his plan together. My son did get real upset at first about not being able to make it. His father then made other plans locally that kind of made up for missing the concert, my son was OK with it. I thank the Lord! Now it's Tuesday, back to school, and last night, which was Monday, Memorial Day night, Xman started acting up again, and I had a feeling that he was going to, because it was the end of the holiday and he had to go to school the next day. I had to call his father and first the prayer line, Xman knocked down my chairs and started swearing and I told him if he didn't stop, I would have to call 911. He didn't care, but after the lady on the Prayer line prayed with me about it, and believe me, I told her just what was happening, so she would know what to pray about. I don't hold back when it comes to prayer, they need to know how to pray about any situation you're having. After she prayed, it all stopped because at first, he didn't want to get in the shower. He came out of his room; told me he was getting in the shower. I went into my room, and I took my shower also, and we both went to bed. The next morning, he woke me up and he was fully dressed and ready for school. Thank you, Jesus, prayer works, Amen!

Now Summer Vacation is on its way, and I can't wait until they're officially out of school which is the 6th of June. One good thing about it is that my son's grades went up and I promised him that I would give him a reward for bringing up his grades. I told Xman he could go to the mall and pick out some clothes he wants. Two days before school let out there was a girl's video that went viral, she's a cheerleader for his high school, it was racist and inappropriate. It was all over the news, two people called me about it. I looked at the news to see it for myself and sure enough, it was true. June 4th, they did have the Superintendent reply to it, he said that he will not have any of this activity going on at any of the schools at all. I was glad to hear this, and how upset he was about it; he also had several people backing him there. My son had told me that they were making racial slurs toward him, some of the bullies. Last year was hell! I know that the Lord is just letting us go through this but not stay in it, I do believe.

Xman's been out of school now for a few weeks, and I'm trying to keep him busy. He wants to go to work, he told me, and get his driver's license, but he has to be prepared for that. I've been looking into some options for him

Attorney Drops the Ball & 911

through the Central Valley Regional Center to prepare him for this. They will connect you with people and places to go to get you started, such as life skills and job opportunities. Xman is now enrolled in camp to keep him busy until a door opens up for him to be placed, and prepared for working etc. However, one of his caseworkers called me, and said that they might have an opening for my son to earn while you learn over the summer. I will pray about it for sure, and about his temper to get it under control. He does pretty good at camp. He had a couple of incidents but nothing major. My son went to see his therapist and he seemed to have a good session, but he did tell the therapist that he didn't understand him.

CHAPTER 8:

The Therapist & Much Prayer

My son has told me that he thinks he hurt the therapist, Dr. N.'s feelings, because the therapist put his head down after Xman said what he said. My son also told me that Dr. N. is too old to talk about things happening in his age group.

Remember I mentioned that I had taken Legal action against the school district for all the things that Xman has gone through at his high school? Then the attorney tells me at the last minute, that she couldn't represent me any longer and to look for someone new. I was very distraught about this, a whole year, (I thought to myself) that she had to tell me. I had been sending them info for the case that had been documented with times, and dates of all the incidences. When I thought we would be getting ready for court, the attorney switched reels on me. I'm looking for a new attorney and praying to get this matter resolved in a timely manner. Not to change the subject but my son Xman said he had a good day at camp yesterday, he said he went swimming twice. I know my son just wants to fit in with his peers, and feel a sense of normality, that's it. I love my son so much; it saddens me to see him struggle. Right now, I'm tearing up just thinking about it. "Lord, I leave this pain all in your hands."

My son saw his therapist the other day, and after his session he tells me that he wants another therapist, "here we go", because his therapist doesn't understand him. I told my son that the therapist is there to listen to you vent, give suggestions to relieve stress etc. I thought Dr. N. was a good fit for

911, Broken. **Give it to God!**

Xman because he's very mellow, and laid back, and listens well, but Xman still wants me to look for someone else. It's always something.

The therapist Dr. N. wrote me a "whomever it concerns" letter about Xman's situation at school, for the school and for attorney purposes and Dr. N. was on point about my son's behavior. I don't know why my son says that Dr. N. doesn't understand him because what he wrote in the letter sounds like he understands him pretty well, and what he's going through. I can give the letter as a document to the next attorney who takes my case. I'm very appreciative of this from the doctor, the information is more than enough. Right now, my son is on his summer vacation, and he's been going to camp which he likes. He can go five days a week if he wants. He swims, plays in the gym, by the way, did I tell you he's a good swimmer, he loves the water. At camp, they also watch movies, and they have structure. He's been going every summer for four years. The lady in charge of the camp, Mrs. B., made Xman a Volunteer, like a helper so that he doesn't have to pay, and he can still do the activities and help out at the same time, and he's learning responsibilities, has a sense of belonging and leadership. Right now, I'm just praying for the best school to go to for his last year as a senior. My son wanted to work over the summer, but he needs more prepping before that happens. However, we do have resources through CVRC, Central Valley Regional Center, but we got started a little late. Xman also needs some other documents before he can get started, and we still need to work on his anger issues. Camp is a little different, it's all fun and games, but to go to work and be told to do certain things will need prayer and therapy, it's very important. I want nothing more than to see my son's success. Xman also likes going to the mall, he has a favorite shop in it that has lots of clothes for teens. Xman was supposed to visit his sister, grandma, uncle and nieces, but he couldn't make it this summer. A lot of stuff came up, and I had some unexpected expenses however, I spoke to his sister, and we plan on doing something for Thanksgiving.

My son is going to a different school this year because of all the drama that went on at his school last year, and the year before that. I've had it with them. I took him out of his old school and transferred him to a new high school for his last year. I spoke to the counselors at the new school, and he's got a very good schedule. No math or science this year because he took it 3 years in a row at his last school so, that's a blessing. Thank God, because they weren't grading him fairly at the other high school which caused him to flare up, especially with math, and that crazy teacher he had that sung in his algebra class. It also got a little racist. I'm happy for the change.

I prayed about all this and let the Lord know to let His will be done, so this must be His will for my son to be able to go to this new high school because he was accepted, and enrolled. Prayer works, now this is the first day of school, and my son doesn't have to get up so early anymore. He can walk to school if he wants, it's so close, and that's what he'll be doing. He got up, started getting ready for school, he has everything he needs for now. Backpack, new utensils, and we went the day before to find out where his classes were located so he wouldn't have difficulties the first day trying to find them. He had four classes the first day. This school's program is a little different, you have four classes a day and eight classes total, so you have one set of four one day, and the next day you complete your second set of four classes which makes eight in total. Xman will have to get used to it, he was a little nervous that morning going to a new school and all. He called me on his break and said that he tried to make friends, but he didn't get a chance to tell me what happened, he had to go back to class. I told him don't try so hard, just relax, be cool, if someone speaks to you respond back. I told him this before he started this school. I also told him this is not a party or social event, its school, you're there to learn, and get up out of there. Friends will come in time, don't force a friendship or relationship ever, because it won't be genuine. I know it's very important to have someone to relate to, and I trust that the Lord will send good people Xman's way to meet. I'm' praying for that.

Xman also had an appointment with his psychologist that same first day, which was good so that he could vent, and get out any anxiety off his chest. Doctors are here for a reason, so we should take advantage of them. The Lord has given them a gift, a lot of them, because their wisdom has given us cures through knowledge, and the skills to operate. God bless our doctors. We haven't been able here lately to make it to church. The church that we were going to, moved to another city and we really need to find another one because it's really too far to drive to. When we go to church it keeps us grounded. Yesterday, my neighbor told me that her house was broken into, and she was only gone for an hour. They also have an alarm, and a sign outside, but it didn't seem to stop the burglars from going into the side of their garage door and taking out two TV's and coming out the main garage door, how bold. That to me is like what they would call a home invasion. How did they know that the alarm wasn't on or when anyone would be back. To be that bold they had to be strapped with guns, or just plain idiots. This is scary, and the neighborhood we live in is pretty nice, all residential. That's why I stay in prayer.

This weekend my son had a flare up, we had just watched a church program on TV that Sunday and after that he spoke to my mother, his grandma, on the phone about how he didn't like the way his father was treating his father's girlfriends. Soon after that, he came in the room where I was, and had a strange look in his eyes, and ran towards me, and swung his fist at me. I had a phone in my hand, I held it up like to let him know if he took one more step towards me, I would have to defend myself. I told him I'm going to call 911 if he doesn't stop, then he said "mom, I'm going back in my room, don't call please", I told him if this keeps up, you'll have to go live somewhere else, I can't keep going through this behavior with you. I called my daughter, and my daughter told Xman she would drive up if he didn't stop, and my mother told him "You just got off the phone with me and talked about how you didn't like to see anyone mistreated like that". I told my son we just got through watching a church program together. My daughter talked to him for a long time. He finally went back to his room, and calmed down because my daughter also told him that she would call the police if she heard that he does it one more time. To top it off, my mother just got back a few days ago from seeing her doctor, and they found a mass on her breast, and they want to do a biopsy on it to make sure it's not malignant. I didn't want her to get upset at all, you see how this affects everyone. My daughter also told me that Xman has been watching things on the Internet and listening to music that has satanic messages in it, as soon as I got off the phone, I started

The Therapist & Much Prayer

praying immediately for any demonic activity to leave the home right now! In the name of Jesus! I also called the prayer line about the situation and so far, he's been OK. I did find out a good thing over the weekend and that was that he made a friend at school last week, a girl, and he told me her name. My mother told me that he told her about the girl also. Thank the Lord!

New day, remember when I told you about the excursion over the weekend with Xman's temper, well so far, he's been doing pretty good this week. When I was talking to my mother and daughter, that day, when all you know what broke loose. I stopped in the middle of a sentence and said aloud "any demonic spirit, and or bondage in this home, I rebuke it in the name above all names, in the name of Jesus, you have to flee right now". I noticed this week that my son took down a lot of pictures off his walls in his room that looked demonic also, he's been coming out of the room wanting to talk. Unlike the usual isolation he does, with a twist of attitude. He's been smiling more and asking questions, leaving and ready for school on time. We finally made it back to our old church. The church had moved a city over, and I thought it would be too far to drive, and that we might have to find another one to attend. I went on and drove the distance this weekend and we made it. The drive wasn't too bad, I tell you what, at this point we just need to go. My son seemed happy he saw a girl from his old high school there, and they talked for a while until the doors opened to go into the main building of the church. The door opened, we went in, and the singing and praising began, they sound so good, I love their singing also. At this church you can come as you are. It's not just a dress to impress. There's also a lot of youth there, and they run lots of equipment, such as camera, preach some, etc. Although the Pastor is around my age, his son preaches too. When we got back from church, my son was doing OK. Now I noticed in church when we were saying a prayer that one of the preachers asked everybody to pray. I didn't hear Xman say anything, and he was standing right next to me. When we were at home, he did OK for a while then he went in his room for a while, came out, this was right before bed and started acting radical and talking about how he doesn't fit in anywhere. He acted like he was going to throw one of my heavy glasses on the floor, but he put it back down. He started swearing a lot and talking about hurting himself again. I called his father up and told him, he talked to him for a while and then I talked to his dad. I told him I think Xman is listening and looking at the wrong things on the Internet. That's what happened last time he was listening to heavy metal and looking at demonic activity on the Internet, and remember his sister mentioned this also, and I've had other family members say the same thing. I also saw one of his screen savers and it looked very demonic. I haven't said anything about this stuff yet because I don't want it to escalate. What I should have done was take him up for prayer, also this weekend I let him color his hair, he seemed very happy with that. He told us that a lot of teens at school do it. I went up to the school while they were getting ready for football practice on Saturday and asked some of the players about colored hair and they told me that they've even done it. I just wanted to make sure it was OK to do it at this new school. I told his dad he could go ahead and get it done. It's a dark purple, and it doesn't look bad at all, he just needs to get a good cut or shape.

On the first day of the week Xman's father finally shows up, he brought over a boxing bag so that when Xman gets upset, he can box it out. I thought it was the best idea besides sliced bread. I thought to myself this could possibly keep him from tearing up the house. He needs ways to take out his frustrations and get some relief. I get it, I also need the same thing sometimes myself. I have noticed that since he's been at this new high school, he's been a little calmer, he sometimes has a little anxiety because it's new, but otherwise, he's been calmer. The staff there seem more laid back and helpful, not so stressful. Now tomorrow he has an appointment with his psychologist. The day of this appointment we found out that the doctor had made an appointment for Xman to see a psychiatrist, so we're just going to go to that appointment instead. This is the Labor Day weekend and I'm very glad that we get an extra day off. I have a lot on my plate at this time.

My mother was diagnosed with a spot on her breast and they're not sure if it's cancer yet, she might have to have it removed, she's up in age in her 80's and lives in another city than I do. I want to be with her, but I don't trust anyone in my home while I'm away. I was thinking of asking Xman's father,

The Therapist & Much Prayer

but I don't even want him in my home while I'm gone. He has a problem with probing through my paperwork, and one time, when I was over at a friend's house, while he was supposed to be watching Xman, I came home to find him and some strange girl in my den asleep together. I immediately had to put them out. The nerve! However, I've been praying for my mother and have her on the prayer list. A very dear friend of hers is going to be with her, and she got an anointing on her, and she has also been interceding for my mother. I know that she'll be alright, I just would like to be there to show my support. At this particular time, I can't take Xman out of school. This particular school really frowns on absences, as a matter of fact, they sent a letter home and also put a message on the phone about it. Plus, he just got there and also, Xman doesn't want to go down where my mother lives, because of her brother, his granduncle. They don't get along well at all. We don't need any strife, especially at this time, just peace.

So far, this week has been going pretty smooth, I just had to take care of my business, oil change, paperwork and so on. Xman has been coming home in a better mood than he used to from his old school. The only thing that really got me upset is my son's money didn't come in, he's on S.S.I, Social Security, and that helps cover our bills since I take care of him and his needs. I was working but I was getting calls constantly from his school for different things, and I would have to take off to pick him up, plus, he also has a lot of appointments. With all that goes on on a daily basis, my mind couldn't focus on working elsewhere. Then my boss where I was working, felt for me and let me work from home because it was too hard, my son might need something or might be going through something. I worked in marketing, and it didn't sound professional with screaming, or any interruptions going on in the background. I could have kept on working from home, but occasionally those things happened with all the noise and all. So, my full-time job is my son. That's how I make my living, I get paid for it, and am able to put food on the table. If you ask me, it's all because of the shots, his immunizations when he was a toddler that caused the Autism. A lot of doctors wrote about it and said that the mercury levels that were in the shots were extremely high and caused the Autism and, that the government released them anyway. I feel for the children, and any parent that has a child with Autism that has to go through this. It's not a joke, and they should get paid for the rest of their lives. The emotional roller coaster that a person or persons has to ride with this horrific disease.

CHAPTER 9:

No Child Left Behind

It's Friday, yesterday I went to his back-to-school night and got to meet most of his teachers, only a couple weren't there, however, I did get to meet all his academic teachers. That was really important to me, after all, this is his senior year, and I want it to be one of his best years in school. I want his GPA to stay at least at a 3.0 because that's where it was before all the drama unfolded at his last school. I also want his teachers to know that I care about his grades and the support he's getting at school, and to see if he even has a good support team working with him. However, it's just now starting so I'm happy to have gone. Most of his teachers said that he is doing pretty good, that he does ask questions if he doesn't understand something, the others said that he was struggling in some of his academics. I got right on it and let them know that he has a lady that is supposed to be working with the teachers in his support class and to please get in contact with her so, if there's anything that their lacking, they'll be on top of it. I don't want him left behind. I know with prayer it will all work out.

That Friday, right before school let out, I went and picked up something to eat from two of his favorite Asian restaurants we normally eat at, and got some tempura there, and the other one, fried rice and spring rolls. I thought to myself since he's had a busy week, and in some classes a hard week, so let me let him know that I care, and that maybe this will cheer him up a bit. I forgot to mention that one day, that past week, his ceramic teacher told me Xman had to leave class because he was having anxiety attacks, due to being overwhelmed from so many students in the class and being new to the school. Right after that, his case worker at the school called me to make an appointment for an I.E.P. meeting which is like I mentioned before, stands for Individual Education Program. This school needs their own assessment, and program in place for him for his last year in high school. Time goes by so fast and when you have a plan in place everybody's in sync with each other, and working together to help him conquer any problems easier that might occur during the year. It also helps to keep your child on track. I really want my son to get his diploma, not a certificate. The certificate doesn't carry the same weight as a diploma, they're not equivalent at all. That's the goal, we'll see how it goes.

This Friday Xman had an appointment with his therapist Dr. N., and it didn't go well. I normally leave and go to the store or something, but this time I didn't, I waited for him to finish. When we first got there the therapist came out and asked me if I wanted to talk to him before the session, and I said yes. I went in, told him that Xman was struggling in his academics and will be having an I.E.P meeting at his school next week to put a plan in place also, that he dyed his hair purple, and cut off his eyebrows. I also had told his case worker at the school the same thing, and that we really need that meeting fast. Now I know that being a teen now days isn't easy, and trying to fit in is a task in itself. I just don't understand a lot of the things they go through on a daily now days. It's been so long ago since I've been in school. After the meeting the therapist came out even before Xman's time was up to tell me that Xman threatened to have him fired, and said some very disturbing things to him. I apologized for that for my son and, the therapist said that Xman thought he was being racially profiled and that he didn't understand him at all, and that he felt like vomiting all over him, the therapist. I was very hurt for Dr. N. because the doctor had told both of us, he was also bullied in school and could relate to my son, he was very calm and soft spoken, that's why I thought it would be a good fit. He looks very conservative, he wears glasses, dresses in slacks and buttoned up oxford shirts with loafers. He's a middled aged guy, I thought to myself maybe Xman needs someone a little younger, I don't know anymore. All I could do was call the prayer line and stand on that. I spoke with a friend of mine, and they told

No Child Left Behind

me to step out of the way and let the Lord do his work. That's what I have to do however, at that same session, the doctor told me that he was going to teach Xman some breathing exercises to calm himself down in a crisis, that's if my son would let him finish the session. They were almost through, but the doctor stopped to tell me these things. I also got a message from the school in a text that said Xman has to dye his hair back to his natural color, and that message came from the Vice Principal. I had thought that it was OK to let him dye his hair after speaking to those football players but, I never got permission from the school. Plus, I don't remember if I mentioned this, but he not only dyed it purple, he then changed it to an eye shocking red, and not a natural red head, but red like a fire truck. They don't allow that at the school. They gave him a time period to change it back, about a week. He also cursed one of his teachers in economics class. I received notification from his case worker at school. When he came home, I was very calm about it, and I told him I knew about it. I asked him to give me his Dr. Dre Bluetooth radio speaker that he listens to. The volume on that thing goes up so high I was kind of glad I wouldn't be hearing that music for a while. I tell you one thing, that little thing makes you think you're in a club as loud as it gets, and I can only imagine what the clubs sound like nowadays, and I'm not trying to find out. I told Xman that he wouldn't be getting it back until he starts being more respectful. I also called the prayer line about his behavior.

Yesterday was the I.E.P. meeting, and before the meeting, I told his father and the Central Valley Regional Center Rep. to meet me there. It's called CVRC, they help families that have children with disabilities to connect them with help and refer you to other facilities that can be an asset to families that are lost for answers. They check with you, and the child on an annual basis, so you know how much progress the child has made. They also come as a witness to the I.E.P. meetings such as this one I just had, to make sure the child is getting a fair share in all of this. Now when a teenager goes into adulthood, they don't just drop the child, they still provide ways to hook up with help such as, places where they can get work training, etc. I invited his case worker from CVRC to be at the meeting, and they will also get a copy of the I.E.P. papers to make sure the school does what they say they're going to do. It's all documented and it's always good to have a witness in your meetings so if anything goes awry, you can refer to the notes or witnesses. The meeting started at 10:30 that morning. I got there at 10:10 and waited in my car making business calls till about 10:20. I went in and spoke to the receptionist at the front desk in the lobby of the school, she found my son's I.E.P. appointment. I sat down and waited for my party of people which was his father, and the case worker from CVRC.

Finally, I see the case worker from CVRC, and another lady walks up to open up the front office to the conference room where the meeting will be held. I however didn't see my son's father yet, and we had spoken on the phone that morning, and said we were both going to get ready and meet up at the school. Now you know I stayed in constant prayer for the victory and favor to fall on this meeting for my son. Believe me when I say it did! because out of the blue everybody showed up, and more. It had to be at least 10-15 people there, all the teachers I requested and more. We all sat down around an oval table, and it begun. His case worker of the school, Mrs. S. was the one leading the meeting and we were in sync with his program. What my main concern was, was that he got enough support so that he doesn't fall behind. I'd also prefer him to get a diploma, rather than a certificate. Now if he gets a certificate, they will work with him until he's 22 years of age on all subjects including his life skills. Such as counting money, navigating through the city, etc., the things that prepare you for living on your own, which is very important. His father finally shows up. When we sat down, when we got there everybody introduced themselves to us and we did likewise. Everyone looked very eager to get started, and they were pretty friendly. The main thing was for me to address his grades, because his academics teachers, on back-to-school night, told me that Xman had been struggling and I was getting worried. I told them that he's coming from another school, and this would be his first year at this school, he doesn't know anyone and he's a senior, so this is crucial. I also let them know that his GPA was at a 3.0 and I'd like it to either, go up but never go lower than that. Now, his school case worker Mrs. S., who was leading the meeting did an assessment on Xman in all his academics and told me that the other

No Child Left Behind

school lied to me about where he's at in his academics, and said that he's quite behind his grade level, which really got to me. I told Mrs. S., the case worker, that when she tested him, he probably wasn't focused, and due to this new environment, he's uncomfortable testing. We went over his test scores, then his father nudged me, and said maybe it would be better if he went for the certificate instead of the diploma. Mrs. S. also said that if he gets the diploma, that they wouldn't be able to help him any further, and said by law, with the certificate, he'd have more support and it would continue until he turned 22 years of age, if needed. I was just concerned about his credits and, if he went to a Junior College, would he be able to make up his credits there, so that he could get his diploma as he goes to college for a degree or, would he just have to quit and work a menial job, that's not what I want for Xman. I don't want to see my children struggling. That's why I know in the Bible it says that you should leave an inheritance for your children's children to give them a chance in life. I believe they also should have good work ethics, and stay busy doing something, and helping people less fortunate than yourself. You know idle time is the devil's workshop. We set a time schedule for Xman to see how he does in school for the next 2 months, to see if he can keep up with this new support team. We all agreed to see how it works so he can stay on the diploma track.

Changing subjects, Xman doesn't want to see his therapist anymore, remember the last session was cut short and Dr. N. wants to teach him breathing exercises to calm him down in a crisis, I felt he really needed that. I will be trying to convince him to go back.

I had been looking for another attorney in my area so that I can complete my lawsuit against the school district at his other high school he was in, because I haven't forgotten all that happened to him there, and it was very wrong, and needs to be addressed properly. There needs to be something done, some justice so that no one else has to go through that ever. After they told me at this new school he's attending now, that they felt the other school lied to me about the level that his academics are at, I'm even more upset and concerned. I called and spoke to the psychologist's secretary, the office manager, and she told me I could have Xman sign a paper at the front desk giving me permission to speak to the doctor on my son's behalf, because now he's turned 18 years of age. I have to have his permission to discuss anything pertaining to him now. That also went for his I.E.P., they had him give verbal permission for me to speak on his behalf there also. After a while we brought him in because he was not in the room of the I.E.P. for a while, because I knew some of the subjects we hit on would be a trigger for him, and possibly shut down the meeting. We let him stay out the first part of it. I do need to speak with his psychologist regarding the case that I've been handling for my son regarding his old school and attach an attorney. It's already been filed by the other attorney, that's a plus. I just need more evidence entered if he's going to get any compensation for damages which he's entitled to, after all, he's been through and I'm doing everything in my power to make sure he does.

The attorney service I'm dealing with wants the psychologist to give an approximate amount of money that he believes it's worth, due to the services Xman is getting, and how much more help he'll need will also determine it. He's still dealing with anger, and suicide issues due to all the occurrences at the school. I called up, left a message to speak with his psychologist, Dr. N., so I can get that info, but first Xman will have to go in and sign the papers to release the info to me on his behalf. That's in the makings and we are on a statute of limitations, so, I have to get it done pretty quick and get that info to the attorney that will be handling the case. Xman didn't feel good the Friday that just passed so he stayed home that day.

Saturday his father finally picked him up, because he needed to recolor his hair back to his natural color and his father had a friend that he knew could do it. The school told him that they can't wear any neon colors, so on Saturday he picked him up and got it done back to his natural color, "what a relief". His natural color looked a lot better to me, it made his skin look clearer and he wouldn't stand out like a sore thumb. That Sunday Xman and I went to the Cheesecake Factory for lunch and had a nice time, we also listened to a church program on TV. That day, a minister that I really liked was on that spoke about faith, and both of us needed to hear that. Sometimes, if we can't make it to church, we will look at it on TV together. Like the

No Child Left Behind

Lord says in Matthew 18:19, if any two of you agree on earth concerning anything that they ask, it will be done for them by My Father in Heaven. After we had a beautiful lunch, we went shopping for Fall clothes and we had a great time together.

Today is Monday, back to our regular routine. Yesterday, after Xman got out of school we went up to his psychologist's office and signed the paper for him to release the info to me, and for me to speak on his behalf. You know, I mentioned earlier in the book that Xman and I both try to read the Bible every morning, except on the weekend, sometimes I might read on Saturday. Even if we don't go to church, I will at least try and find a minister on TV and listen to the Word. It helps us so much, and due to that, the other day Xman started quoting things in the Bible, and saying that these are the end times, and talking about all the demonic activities that he sees on the Internet and telling me what they mean. He told me that in Florida, he saw on the internet, that they have children's books that they're introducing Satanism to little kids. He also said he sees a lot of teens wearing the pentagram symbol, and doing satanic rituals on the internet as well, and sacrifices. He told me he doesn't trust hardly anyone now. He did tell me that he is not into that, which is a big relief to me as a parent.... Xman did bring up through the week that he got behind in about three of his classes, so I told him to make the support team print out his work and also, go to them and have them get in touch with me because we're too late in the game to regress. I have to stay on top of this, it's very important especially now that he's in his senior year. Xman also has to put in his work as well, to keep up.

I received a phone call from the attorney service letting me know to send in my paperwork. They needed the summons and complaint against the school info, for them to assign me an attorney to represent this case. That's what I'm working on now.

Over the weekend Xman went to the mall. I told him that he needs to get out of the house and be around some people so, I took him to the bus stop, and he caught the bus there and stayed most of the day. He normally gets something to eat there and buys himself a shirt or something and looks through the shops. That was Saturday and on that day I rested. We made it to church this Sunday, and it was good. The Pastor's son preached, and he hit some crucial topics, he read out of 2 Kings 6:1-7 and applied it to our lives today. You might want to read it yourselves. The pastor's son was speaking about the sons of the prophets and Elisha when they went to cut down trees and one of them lost the head of the axe he had borrowed. You have to read the whole story for yourself, but the pastor's son said it's just like today, when you lose something or didn't do well at something, and start to question yourself, and have a sense of low self-esteem. He said that sometimes in life, you will have those issues, but the Lord will allow it to make your loss turn into gain. Sometimes He'll shut a door that you think you should of went right through, to show you later on, that he has something better in store for you, so in actuality you haven't lost anything. The Lord just knew that that wasn't the best thing for you. It was an awesome sermon, and everyone needs to know that the Lord is working behind the scenes, and we just have to trust in His work. After church we went out to eat at a restaurant down the street from our house which was very good, they gave us so much food we couldn't even finish it all. We had a good conversation, and everything. God is good. Also, over the weekend I got to tell a lot of my family and friends about First Fruit Offerings. It's in the Bible, it's about the Jewish Holiday's and giving during that time the Lord really recognizes it and blesses you, and your families dearly. I know every time I've given during it, I've been supernaturally blessed. I forgot one other thing that the pastor's son said, he also said to learn the importance of what you're connected to, like people. God will send people to you, in your life, to push you forward. Also, people to challenge you. It can make you stronger.

Today is the beginning of a new week. This week I was informed that during an assembly at Xman's school they were speaking on school violence, and if there ever became an attack on the school, they were telling the teens what precautions to take. I got a call from the V.P. of Xman's school, and they told me to call ASAP. I called the school, and they told me that Xman had made a comment during the assembly saying that if there was a shooting, he wouldn't use a table or something else to guard himself, he would fight back or shoot back, that was what some of the girls claim that was said

No Child Left Behind

during the assembly. I spoke to my son, and he said he didn't say anything about shooting, he said he would have to protect himself the best way he knew how. He also told me that he was misunderstood. Mighty funny, that all this was said after I had requested another I.E.P. meeting, due to 3 of his academic classes he was failing in, after we had not so long ago, had the I.E.P. meeting. I was reassured that his academics teachers were going to be interacting with his support team if he was behind or needed retesting so that he wouldn't fall behind. When I heard how far behind he was, I contacted the school and spoke to the lady of the support group, Mrs. S., and she told me that she'd been working with him more than anyone else. I said if that's the case, why is he failing in 3 classes with all this support, and she told me that my son wasn't going to his support groups, and like I said, the teachers and support all know his grades and where he's at so there to me, is no excuse for him to be that far behind. I also told Mrs. S. that I do have a lawsuit with the school district for neglect and abuse. Then Mrs. S. told me she felt threatened, and I told her I don't know why, but we do need another I.E.P. meeting to nip this in the bud, with my son in it too, to make sure we get back on track.

This week I heard from my dad, and I told him about my court date coming up soon, and I told him I would really like for him to be a part of it just for support. My dad then called me back and said he had mailed me some info that I might need for it and attorneys that represent these kinds of cases. I said great. I also got hooked up with an attorney and have an appointment coming up soon.

Today I have a meeting with the school to reiterate the support plan we have in place. We had the meeting at school. When I first walked in you could tell everyone was anxious to get this over with. I spoke first, it was about 7 or 8 people there, his father showed up also, and I let them know my concerns about his 3 academic classes he was failing in, and his father had pulled up the information on the screen of his phone that shows his grades, and how many assignments he's missing. I questioned each teacher to find out the accuracy of the info on the phone screen. The first teacher was his English teacher, and in his class my son was missing 7 assignments and Mr. B.

his English teacher told me that Xman was really struggling in his class but was giving his best effort to stay on track, he also said that he didn't utilize the tutoring time that he had for him at lunchtime. His other class that we were concerned about was his Economics class which on the portal, said he was missing one assignment, and he had an "F" in that class as well. I spoke to Mr. O., another teacher, and he said he was struggling and wasn't coming to be tutored on time either, so I questioned that teacher, and asked why he was failing when he only was missing one assignment, and then, Mr. O. told me that he just retested Xman, and that he hadn't put in his assignments into the system yet, but that Xman had a very low score on most of his work, and some incomplete work that needed to be finished. I could tell that everyone was doing everything they could, even his caseworker was letting me know that it was getting overwhelming for him as well. There was one last teacher we were going to hear from, and I was already exhausted mentally from all of this, and that was Mr. M. his American Government teacher.

CHAPTER 10:

New Psychiatrist & Harmful Meds

didn't want to even hear any more so I asked what our options were, and both the English teacher and the Economics teacher said they would still help him at lunch, but I could see the look on Xman's face, and his gestures, that he had just had it. He was overwhelmed. I asked about the certificate, and they told me that with the certificate he would get all the help he needed, even extra help, and if he needed extended time, he would also get that too, up until 22 years of age plus, life skills such as cooking, counting money, navigation skills, etc. He also would be able to graduate with the rest of the seniors. Then Xman could also get his diploma later at Adult School and possibly get a degree and or go to a four-year University. His father and I agreed on the certificate. We got started that same day and got all the paperwork signed. Xman also agreed, it was a big relief, I was a little hesitant at first but after adding up all the facts it was best.

Yesterday I picked up Xman early from school, he finally got his appointment with his new Psychiatrist, Dr. B. As we were driving to the office Xman was telling me about Senior Picture Day at school, they went on a field trip that morning, all the seniors, and took pictures at their football stadium. He said he enjoyed himself, but he did say that some of the teens were acting a little aggressive and pushing people to get to their friends to talk to, or take a picture with them. As we got closer to the doctor's office Xman started telling me he didn't want to go. He wanted to go back home, it was like something came over him and it started playing tricks with his mind. He even went as far as to pound on the car door while I was driving. It was so hard to get the appointment in the first place, and I knew if we missed this appointment, it would be a long time before I could get another one. I had to make it, so I kept on driving through all the drama and praying at the same time. We finally made it. We went in the office, and they handed me a whole lot of paperwork to be filled out since this was his first visit. It was a lot of papers, I got most of them filled out. Xman was getting claustrophobic, and pushing the table while I was writing, further away from me with his feet. There was another mother and child in the office with us trying to play like they weren't paying attention, but you could see the expression on the child's face that he knew something wasn't quite right. I tried getting that paperwork filled out as fast as I could. Finally, they called Xman's name, thank God! We went back to see the doctor, the psychiatrist in his office. The doctor was a middle-aged man with silver hair of an Indian descent, mid weight and about 5'10" to 5'11" in height, very well dressed, nice slacks and long sleeve shirt, very distinguished.

We all sat down, the doctor had out his computer, he wanted to go over my family health history and Xman's also, so we did. I told the doctor about Xman's behavior patterns to see what kind of meds were out to help with him with his anger issues, and he gave me 4 different names, and described how they would affect him; he even told me some of the side effects he might experience. We went down the list of these drugs, and agreed on one that he told me could give him tremors, and his eyes rolling back in the head if it had any side effects on Xman but, he also said that 90% of the people that were taking this one drug never experienced that. I had Dr. B. call in the prescription to our pharmacy, then we made another appointment to see him and left.

As we were driving home, I was thinking about those side effects and went straight home. I didn't pick up the medicine, instead, I went and picked us up a pizza dropped off my son and left the house to digest all of that. I came to the conclusion of going to church and having Xman prayed over, but before that happened, I called my son to let him know to call his dad, and see if over the weekend, he could pick him up, because I needed a break just to unwind. I ended up going across town to see a couple of acquaintances to

New Psychiatrist & Harmful Meds

talk to and brought a bottle of wine to go with it. At this point I was beside myself; I knew I shouldn't have been drinking but I didn't care, I was an idiot. I ended up spending the night out. I knew I needed to go home, so the next day I went home. I got in the next day and got on the phone, and spoke to my mother about the doctor's session, because she's always concerned about my son and his wellbeing. I cleaned up a little and when I got there my son was still out with his dad, so I waited for him to come in. He finally came on in, and I locked down the house and went to bed.

CHAPTER 11:

The Pastor on Fire For Jesus!

Next day was Sunday and I knew I needed Jesus, so I got up, started listening to my ministry programs on TV and I felt compelled to go to church. I started my routine looking for what I was going to wear. I took a shower, woke up Xman and let him know what service we were going to, made us breakfast and started getting ready. That day we went to the second service which started at 11:00 am, we got there right as the first service was leaving. As I was parking, I was praying and thanking the Lord that we made it. We both needed the Word and to fellowship with the people that had our backs. When we sat down, I felt right at home, my peace came back. My son Xman even looked comfortable. Then the singers came out and they sang some of my favorite songs, and you could feel the anointing in the House of the Lord. Then to top it off, out came one of my favorite pastors, a young guy around his mid-thirties on fire for Jesus! He started preaching and touched on so many important things we needed to hear, for example, when he spoke about that as a child his father wasn't in the home. He had got around the wrong crowd of people and started doing things he had no business doing, and told us that he was in Special Ed. Classes, which my son has experienced, and said he went through some difficult times trying to fit in. My son really needed to hear that, because he's not the only one in Special Ed., and that you're going to have trials and tribulations, but there is still a God, and He knows what you're going through and He will never leave you or forsake you. He also spoke to all the single parents because his mom was head of his household, like me as well, and gave us singles a lot of encouragement to not give up because the Lord knows your issues and has your back. I couldn't stop crying, he touched on so many things I needed to hear, and you could tell that my son was listening too. My son started clapping at the points he was making that he agreed with. Xman even started to get into the music afterwards. I was so thankful to the Lord, He's always right on time. When we left, I went to buy us some burgers and went home. When I got in the house, I immediately called my mother and let her know we made it to church. I told her about how we both enjoyed it so much, and how my son received the message. My mother told me that she also watched some of the ministries on TV and that the Lord has a way of getting a message to you, no matter where you're at, that you need to hear. She is so right, Praise God! We also went up for prayer when the message was over.

CHAPTER 12:

The Case & The Psychologist

This Wednesday, I had a meeting with a new attorney. My appointment was at 9am, I got there, and the receptionist took me into the conference room they had, and had me fill out paperwork, also pay a fee of $150.00 for the consultation. The attorney came in the room dressed very well, a middle-aged man with salt and pepper hair, very nice. We shook hands and got down to business. He asked me to give him some insight on what the case was about. I told him about my son versus the school district because of bullying and neglect. I let him know about the last attorney and how she wasn't local, and that I could never reach her on the phone, but she did file my summons and complaint with the Superior Court, but we went our separate ways. Then the attorney asked if he could read what was filed and I gave him all the court documents also, filled him in on how my son's grades had dropped due to all this. I also told him he's now seeing a Psychologist and a Psychiatrist. I showed him the meds that they had prescribed to my son, also let him see what the Psychologist wrote about his condition which he never had before, depression, isolation and suicidal tendencies, etc. The attorney went over all the paperwork and told me he'd get back to me soon. I gave him the court date and let him know the Statue of Limitations and that it was coming up real soon. He asked me if I was a single mother and I let him know yes, I was and he said would I be doing this on a contingency basis, I told him yes. He said it is a very expensive case, and I told him I felt so, because my son went through hell at that school. We even had to change schools, and at the new school, they're telling me that the old school lied about his GPA being at 3.0, and that he might have to go on certificate status instead of getting a diploma. Which the old school told me he was on diplomacy status. I'm very upset. I've already prayed that the Lord intervene in this matter so, I'll get over being upset, and let go, and let God! The attorney told me he would let me know what's next and I left his office.

On the way home I stopped at the market to go big grocery shopping and then went home. I have another appointment with my son's Psychologist after school today that we haven't seen for a while due to Xman acting very harsh with him the last time he had his visit. Xman told me he didn't want to go back again, but I finally convinced him to go. When I picked him up from school he started to complain about his appointment. I told him to just calm down and let the Psychologist know how he felt, but to give him another chance. We got there and Xman signed in and they give him most of the time a paper to fill out about how you're feeling, so they know where you're at in your feelings. He filled out the papers, and gave them back to the receptionist, then they called the Psychologist Dr. N. out. I told the doctor I'd like a word with him before Xman went in, and he said sure. So, I went in spoke to him about the last session they had and asked him what happened, he was brief. He told me Xman put him on notice to stop assuming stuff. Then I went out and Xman went in. I was praying while he was in there that everything would go okay. The doctor told me to call back on Monday and let him know if Xman is going to stay with him as a patient or go with another doctor and we left.

This weekend we didn't make it to church, but we watched it on TV together and again one of my favorite ministers was on. He spoke on favor, the favor of God over your life. We both needed to hear that. When you have the favor of God, the Lord promotes you, and other people can see it. Also, you might get haters because they wonder "Why You and Not Them", but that's how the favor of God works. I prayed with the minister for that favor to fall on us. It's supernatural. That's what we need. That Sunday we went to lunch together and the devil tried to get us to argue, but it stopped quick! The Lord intervened and we made it to the restaurant and had a nice

The Case & The Psychologist

time. We laughed and talked, and had a good lunch. Xman really opened up, I was so thankful.

Today was a pretty good day. I went to look at furniture and came up on a good deal. My son got off to school good, I didn't have any morning problems. He also went to see his dad today and he seemed pretty happy about that. Xman had told me this morning before he left to school that for me not to worry about picking him up from tutoring at school, that he would walk home. I was very happy but later that day Xman's dad came to get him, and they had been gone for quite a while. When he returned, I spoke to Xman and he kind of snapped at me and went straight to his room. I went to his room to ask him what was wrong, and he started telling me to go away, I heard him cursing. I called my mother and asked her would she call him and talk to him, and she told me yes but when she called, she told me he didn't pick up. I got my phone, called my mother, and told Xman she was on the phone, he opened the door and threw my phone against the wall, and broke it. He put a hole in the closet door in the hallway. I called his father, asked him why Xman is so upset, and he told me he didn't know why. I asked his dad to please talk to Xman, because he's acting like he has a bad spirit over him. He finally got on the phone with his dad then we got into a screaming match, because I was very upset about my phone and the hole in the wall. His father heard us on the phone, and said he was coming over. He got there and spoke to Xman. I guess he told him to apologize so that's what he did. Then he finally told me what the real problem was, which was a teacher at his school, Mrs. L., in one of his classes that gave him an assignment to do, but he didn't understand what she wanted, and both the teacher and him got frustrated. Xman told me he didn't swear at her or anything he just held it in, that's how come he exploded at me. I gave him a sleep aid, told him to go to his room and calm down. Tomorrow I will address this with his teacher, just go to all the other classes, and talk to your counselor at school during Mrs. L's class, until I have a chance to talk to her.

This morning, I kind of woke up in a bad mood, because my dog I have ran around the corner and I couldn't see her, but I could hear her barking, and also another dog barking. I didn't know what was going on. I ran out of the house, called my dog Zoe's name, this was about 5 in the morning. I still was half asleep, I was really sleepwalking. I ended up hitting my big toe on a tree stump and cracking the nail on my foot, straight down the middle. It was so painful, it started bleeding. I was trying to find a Band-Aid to wrap it up. I finally got the dog in the house and put her in the backyard with her food, to get her out the way while I got Xman up to get ready for school. I had to call the prayer line; I couldn't take it anymore. Once I did that I went and woke up Xman and he was already up. He must of heard the dog and I, he asked what happened and I told him. He didn't give me any problems, he started getting ready for school. I also read my bible and he did too, the house calmed down, thank you Jesus!

This Monday morning, the time had gone back, I woke up in pretty good spirits. I watched my gospel program on TV and read my Bible. I always leave my Bible on the kitchen counter for my son to read, after I have read. I try to pick out something for him that pertains to the situations we're going through, I try to find something to lift him up, it just depends, sometimes the Lord will just pick it out for me. I'll open the Bible and there will be something meant for us to read. God is so awesome! I also pray for the peace of Israel; it is very important. In Genesis 12:3, it tells us if you bless the Jews you'll be blessed and if you curse them, you will be cursed. Right now, antisemitism is on the rise, so we really need to help them as much as we can. I love them, they've helped me so much in my life, in school, on jobs, and taught me a lot. God bless them!

This weekend I bought the spackle for the holes in my walls, and bought a new phone, and let Xman know that I am taking it out of his allowance. I also spoke to his counselor and told him about the situation with Xman, and I spoke to my son's dad, and he told me that we can't keep changing his classes. Also, the counselor said we would have another I.E.P. to change it, meaning that everyone would have to be pulled out of class, teachers and all. I spoke to Mrs. L., the teacher whom my son was referring to, she told me that he doesn't complete his tasks that she gives him, and as she explained, they don't sound that difficult, so I'm not changing his class. Plus, this is what you call a transitional class, that means that it prepares you for the

The Case & The Psychologist

outside world, like life skills, and he needs that. Right now, they're working on resumes. He needs all this and some, especially counting money so he won't get cheated.

CHAPTER 13:

First Fruit Offerings

This week has been ok for Xman and I, he still sometimes curses but it's getting a little better. I've been very joyous because I got new furniture in and I saved $1,700 dollars on it, it's all because of Jesus. Believe me when I say this, remember when I told you about when you bless the Jews you'll be blessed, well that's what happened, it's called First Fruit Offerings, the Jewish fall holidays, Feast of Trumpets (Rosh Hashanah), Day of Atonement, and Feast of Tabernacles or Sukkot. These Feast start in September, that's the beginning of the Jewish feasts. It's all in the Bible, and I put the money in what you would call good ground, meaning a ministry that Preaches the Word! Straight out of the Bible, and to help the Jewish people get back to their homeland, Israel, and for others in need. God opened the windows of Heaven, and has been blessing me ever since. Things that didn't work on my car started working. Just miracles, Amen. I love the Lord! My daughter called me today and told me that she also received a miracle. I told her that it probably was because of the fall feasts First Fruit Offering that my mom and I gave during the Jewish holidays. My daughter told me that they had a bidding day for new openings for the days and hours on her job, and that someone had told her not to even bid because she was a new hire, like she didn't' have to bid. When she went in to work that next day, three of the main bosses were sitting all together and called my daughter over to speak to her, and asked her where were her bids, she told them what that person told her, the one that said she didn't have to bid and not to worry about any bidding. The three bosses then told my daughter that she could pick out her own days and hours she wanted to work and she did, and my daughter got what she picked, and her weekends off as well. Now that's a miracle!

This Sunday, we made it to a new Bible Study and Xman enjoyed it. It was small but he even interacted with the pastor and other people, what a blessing that was as well. Praise God!

CHAPTER 14:

Flare Ups & Apologies

This weekend started off a little rough because I got a call from the school, an automated call stating that Xman wasn't in his 5th period, and I was concerned about it. I called my mother, told her, then I had decided not to say anything at first because it was our weekend and I didn't want to rock the boat, but I thought about it, and decided that I shouldn't let it go, I need to address this while it's fresh, so I did, and like it's happened before, he blew up. I wasn't thinking correctly, because I should of remembered that's what happens when he's already upset. That's probably why he either went to class late or left early or didn't go at all. There's something happening in that class that he doesn't want to talk about. Me as a parent sometimes forgets his processing as a teen and my bad timing, so he blew up about it when I asked him. I told him I was going to call 911 if he didn't stop, because he started to pound on the wall. I also told him that I was going to call his dad. At this point, he started telling me not to call 911 and I told him if they take him this time, I'm not getting him out. He stopped for a while, all of a sudden, the phone rang, I had been praying for the Lord's help. It was my daughter on the other end of the line. I told her what had happened, she asked to speak with him, she calmed him down a little and when I got back on the phone with her, she said to me "mom why did you mention this now, you know how he gets", I really wondered myself. I should have waited, because I really didn't know how his day went. These are some of the things you must remember while dealing with this horrific disease, Autism. You must remember they process things a little differently. What other people are able

911, Broken. **Give it to God!**

to talk through, sometimes they're not able to, and it can be very difficult for them to explain, which can frustrate them, and cause them to blow up. I felt so stupid the way I handled the matter. I even called the prayer line as always and had them pray with me.

I ended up leaving that night because I just didn't want any flare ups. I ended up over a friend's house and had some wine. I ran from my problems to the bottle, which was not the best thing to do, I couldn't stop crying, I was frustrated myself. I stayed out until the wee hours of the morning and then came home while he was sleeping. I didn't know what to expect that morning but, while I was at my friend's house, she had put on praise music, and another person I knew was there that I wasn't particularly excited to see, because they owed me money that they took one time from me, and never gave it back. They apologized, and I expected one was due to me. After that, then we all started talking about the Lord and His goodness. I felt a lot better. I came home, and when Xman woke up we talked. I made breakfast, we ate together, and we made up and gave each other a hug. We both felt a lot better, that was Saturday morning, then he told me that he spoke to his dad, and that he was going to pick him up and take him to get his hair done. I cleaned up that day and laid back down because I was drained from the night before. I was also waiting on my bed that I bought to be delivered, and it was. I was so happy that I could finally sleep in my own room. I ended up getting out later that afternoon, and going to Macy's, and bought myself a comforter for my bed. It looks so pretty. I also pulled out a comforter set that I got Xman last Christmas that's just like new, only had it on his bed one time, and he'll feel a lot better when we put it on his bed. I'm going to also paint his room and freshen it up for him. That will make him feel better too. I love my son. That Sunday we weren't able to make it to our church, but we had church at home, and it was good. We listened to a man that talks a lot about the youth, and the message was about listening to the wrong voices, and people in your circle that could cause you to fall, but getting around wise people. People with an anointing on them, with wisdom. We both needed to hear that. It also brought peace in the home.

CHAPTER 15:

Superior Court

This week so far has been going pretty good. I had my home painted and I got new furniture. The Lord has truly blessed me. I also went to court yesterday, this was for Xman's case with the school district. I was a little nervous, but I had been speaking to an attorney and with his assistant, they reassured me that I didn't need anyone to represent me for this particular court appearance. So, I dropped off the painter and went downtown to court. Now you know anytime you go downtown to any city, the parking and one-way streets can drive you crazy. I was driving and trying to find the Superior Court down there. Finally, I found it. I thought to myself, now parking time, can we find a parking place, or is that asking too much. I remembered I didn't have much change so how is this going to unfold. I found the address and found a parking lot. There sat a couple in the car as I was pulling up into a parking stall next to them. I asked them if they had any change, the girl on the passenger side handed me some quarters, and didn't even ask for any dollar bills for the change she gave me. There was a guy there that told me all about the parking situation there and said, "you better have enough, because they will surely ticket you here". So, then I asked him if I could give them some money for some more change, and then the girl in the car passed me some more quarters. Then the guy says, "why don't you just park in this spot that I'm in, because I have at least 2 ½ hours on the meter here, and I'll park in your spot because were leaving soon". I said okay, so we exchanged parking places and I put the rest of the change in his meter. I had almost 3 ½ hours left. I then told them thank you, and left to go into court. I thought about what had just happened, and they must have been angels, because nowadays, who do you know that just gives away money without asking for something in return. Who does that? To me it was a miracle, across from where I needed to go downtown where parking is horrific, and someone not only pays you for your parking place, but also gives up theirs! How amazing!

I went inside the Superior Court building where all the sheriffs were standing around by the belt conveyer where you put your belongings through and did that and asked them the way to the elevator. Got on, went to the 4th floor, got off and there was my court room right next to the elevator. I was about 45 minutes early. I went in anyway, and gave my info and sat down, and waited for it to start. There sat a young man bailiff and that's the guy I gave my court papers to, and he located my name. Then I went and sat down, and he also gave me my number in line which was #57, now let me remind you that I had been praying for this day to come, and I didn't have an attorney representing me anymore after the last one. Attorney V., however, she did file the paperwork for me, and I had been speaking with other firms but hadn't got anyone yet. Let's just say "I left it all in God's hands", He was orchestrating all this. The attorney I wanted hadn't told me yet if they were going to represent me, we just had a consultation and I gave his office all my paperwork that was filed. His assistant helped me as far as telling me what to say when I got there, because they wanted to push out the date, because I needed more time for discovery and to prepare, and to attach an attorney to the case.

I saw all the other attorneys suited down and giving their info to appear before the judge to discuss what they were there for. I sat quietly looking and observing everything like I was told to do by the attorney's office assistant, and to wait for my turn to speak. I was line #57 to speak and a lot of things had changed from the times I'd been to court before such as, the new telephone system where the client, and the attorney and judge, speak out loud over this computerized system about their case. When the judge came out and started calling out the line numbers, and most of them were phone calls over that new system they use, the judge would listen to the case and give

Superior Court

the appropriate order depending on each case. I was almost the last case to be heard. I'd say I was there about 2 ½ hours before being heard, so I had time to take notes, to tell the judge what I was told by the attorney's assistant, and what to say to get the extension I needed. When I was heard, I told the judge that I needed more time to prepare, and for discovery for my case, and he gave it to me, and also wished me a Happy Thanksgiving. I was elated with joy to have gotten this over with for now. Now I had more time to plan.

CHAPTER 16:

Thanksgiving Holiday

That evening I came in, Xman and I kind of got into it. I ended up leaving and went over a friend's house to vent again. I stayed almost until morning then we came back to my house, and she washed some clothes, and we watched TV and went to sleep. I told her that Xman and I need to be in church this Sunday and if she wanted to go, she could. So, the next morning I got up, started getting ready to go to church when I remembered that my taillight was out and I didn't want to get pulled over so I told my friend that we would have to stop at an auto place before we went so, we all were ready to go. We were running late, and I really wanted to go to my home church, which was in the next city over, but we didn't have much time. I stopped at an AutoZone, got a guy there to help me put in my taillight and the light worked but, it was too late to make it to my home church, so we ended up having to go to a church a little closer which Xman and I went to a couple of Sundays ago that I spoke about earlier for Bible Study. When we got there, I saw people leaving and I thought we had missed the service and I asked the people coming out there and they thought I meant their church, but it was the other church in the same complex I was speaking about. At first, I thought that we had missed the service altogether, but I had remembered that it started later about 10:45 am, it was around 10:00 am so I still had time. We hugged some people from the other church and found our church, and let those people know that there is another church in the same building that we go to, that started a little later, we made it. Praise God!

911, Broken. **Give it to God!**

Over the holiday, I went shopping and I picked up another TV, and some pictures for my home, so when my grandkids come over, they can have their own TV to watch and play games on. I also got Xman's room cleaned up real good. Now his room is painted, dusted, and it looks real nice. This is the Thanksgiving holiday, and I cooked a turkey with all the trimmings. I had invited the painter over for dinner, because I knew where he was, and he really didn't want to be there. He came over and ate at my house, he was homeless and trying to make some money, a very nice guy. I let him sleep in our den until the morning and then dropped him back off at the place he was at. My son had a fit about it and called the painter all kinds of names, he also tore my Bible up, this was before I dropped the painter off. It was very embarrassing. Thank God the painter was there otherwise I would have had to end up calling 911. I spoke to my mother about this, and she said she would speak to my son, and she did, and told him that everyone needs a friend, and that's your mother's friend, and you can't be mad if she wants to help someone, or has company every now and then, and she also told him that he needs a friend to hang out with too. Just like Barbara Streisand's song says, "People Who Need People, Are the Luckiest People In The World". Xman needs a friend himself to invite over every now and then and go out with. Not isolation all the time. Anyway, left that day with my friend. I forgot to mention what the argument was about; it was about his grades. Xman and I were having breakfast in the kitchen, and I asked him what his grades were, and he told me C's and D's. All this time I'm thinking he's brought them up, because he's been going to tutoring, plus, he's now in modified classes. When he dropped that bomb on me, I got upset and it escalated from there.

This new week we had a behavior program I.E.P. for Xman. There were some concerns about some behaviors in a couple of classrooms of his. It was with his Art teacher that he has to use shears in her class, and that he had the shears pointed to his face poking himself with them, not to the point of bleeding, but the mere fact that he had them pointed to his face was a concern. Xman was in the meeting, and he explained that he would never use them to hurt himself or anyone else. The next teacher that we spoke to was

Thanksgiving Holiday

his transitional teacher Mrs. L. She said Xman hit a girl in the head, and we were all thinking, was it with his fist, but it was with the beanie he wears sometimes on his head. Xman then said that he apologized but they wanted a written statement from him to apologize as well. I also saw that his grades had dropped some more, and we discussed that, Xman kept saying at least I'm passing, and we all tried to tell him that a D is a second away from a fail, I told him I know that he's capable of doing better and that his grades need to be brought back up. We put a plan in place, also because some of his teachers said that he doesn't complete his work, and he'll start complaining. I mentioned that he needs to first complete the task, and then get a break for 5-10 minutes. They also mentioned that he likes to leave the class and go talk to his school counselor or school psychologist, and he can't stay out of class like that, or he'll miss out on what he's supposed to be doing. We arranged a time that would be once a week to see the school psychologist, or one of the mentors at school. I left pretty satisfied with the meeting. We all seem to be on the same page. The next day my son told me he apologized to everyone including the girl that he hit with the beanie. Before I went to the meeting, I had called the prayer line and I prayed for favor, and for the Lord to take control of the meeting. All and all, we ended up with a good plan in place for Xman, my son, that's all that matters and that he learned a lesson and humbled himself. That's how God works! Amen. The day after, I took my son's radio away and put it up. When he came in from school, he asked me if I took it and I told him yes, until he brings his grades up and shows more effort. I know my son is capable of making better grades. He's come too far to turn back now.

We didn't do much over the weekend, it was raining. I love the rain. I just went out for a little while to run some errands. I went to the grocery store and Home Depot to get a toilet for my son's bathroom. The other toilet is no good. My son did talk to his father, and he was pretty upset about the I.E.P. His father came to it, and got upset about the way Xman was cursing and being disrespectful in front of everybody to say the least! His father did call him out of the meeting to get him straight, and when they came back in, he acted a little better. His father had called me and told me that his blood pressure had shot up real high after the I.E.P. meeting. This is very serious. Xman never had an attitude like this before with people. He was always a people's person. On Sunday we listened to a minister on TV, we had church at home. The message was that you have to change your mind and change the way you think in order to change any bad habits. That is so true, it was the perfect message for the both of us. The Word heals! After that, I made us a big pot of gumbo for dinner with French bread, and blueberry muffins for dessert. It turned out to be a peaceful day.

This Monday was ok. I called the prayer line and prayed for my week. My son has been doing a lot better with his cursing although, he still brings up some challenging life issues that are sometimes hard to answer but through the guidance of the Lord, He helps me. My son and I are also listening to each other more. God is awesome! His sense of humor amazes me. I thought about something that the Lord did and how He got my attention and just started laughing out loud, it was so funny. I think about how hard-headed I am sometimes, you have got to give the Lord His props on how he has to handle all these crazy people in the world, and all the different circumstances they go through. It's mind blowing. Godly wisdom is what we all need to make the right decisions, because some things you can't take back once you've made the wrong decision.

I called the school yesterday to speak to Xman's counselor Mr. V. and I explained to him the grades that Xman told me he had. I told his counselor that this is not acceptable. I also told him that finals are coming up, and that my son needs all the info to study on finals, and any assignments that are not complete need to be completed, because since we had the I.E.P., I noticed that 1 or 2 grades had dropped where they should have improved. I'm very concerned about this. I remembered one of his teachers in the I.E.P. meeting responded a little hostile when we were speaking with her about Xman's grades in her class, and how he was doing. I noticed that in that particular class, his C dropped to a D. Mr. V. told me that he would email all his teachers and find out what he's missing, and check on any final studies for Xman that can help him for testing and would get back to me about it either that afternoon or the next morning. I'm just waiting to hear from him.

Thanksgiving Holiday

Yesterday, I called Xman's school, spoke to Mr. V., he said he emailed all his teachers about Xman's work and any incomplete assignments and about any studying on finals. He tried to explain each teacher's comments to me about Xman and I asked him to save his breath, and if he sends anything home with him, I will see that he studies it. I also told Mr. V. to please make sure that Xman completes and hands in all his work on time, and if it's not finished, to make sure he finishes it. Mr. V. reassured me that he would get with Xman and check it all out. Thank you, Mr. V. You know what I did after that, of course, I called the prayer line. When Xman came in at dinner I asked him if he spoke with Mr. V., he said yes, yesterday. I asked him what he said, Xman said he told him that Mrs. S. would help him. That was his school caseworker. What bothers me is that he never started anything yet, meaning working with him yet, and didn't speak to him today at all. It's now, all in God's hands. I'll check back that's all I can do at this point. I spoke to my daughter, and she told me that finals are next week.

This is about to be the Christmas break and I told Xman if he brings his grades up, he'll have a great holiday. I got a call while I was finishing up making my Christmas cards. Xman told me he had got in some trouble at school with one of the aides that was helping him with his assignments. I asked him what happened, and he told me that she was nagging him as he was trying to work and correct his mistakes. Now I don't know if he was getting distracted, and she thought he wasn't getting anything done on time or what, but he told me that he cursed her out, and then apologized. These are sometimes some of the signs you get from Autism, frustration and a quick temperament, but the cursing is not acceptable! He also said I would be receiving a call from someone at the school, and I did, the V.P. called and told me something Xman said, and he would be on detention during lunch. I told the V.P. to give him his incomplete work while he's in there so he can complete it. I didn't know what to expect when he got home but he was mellow. I remembered I prayed about his attitude. When I asked him to do his chores, he did them without a question. He also told me he had homework. God is great! I also gave my son a pep talk to let him know that it's not over yet, and don't give up. You've come too far to stop now. I told

911, Broken. **Give it to God!**

him that he can do anything he puts his mind to, and I know he can catch up, and graduate on time with the other students in his grade. I know what my son is capable of and he's smart, he just needs to apply himself. With the Lord's help, he'll make it.

Mr. V. sent a plan home for Xman over the weekend to follow to help him and his grades get better. Xman was getting too distracted, and his confidence was being attacked. Now when he tests, he can go to a room by himself so he won't get distracted and he can retest if he needs to plus, he has more support. Xman had almost gave up before this. He had gotten so stressed that Tuesday morning we had a bad argument just to get him to go to school. He threw a basket at me that hit me upside my head, and the basket wasn't empty. It had a lot of heavy stuff in it. I was overwhelmed. I told Xman I was going to call 911 if he didn't go to school. I started crying and he started apologizing, but he still didn't want to get ready for school. Finally, I called the prayer line and told them what had happened, Xman walked in as I was on the phone crying, to listen and hear who I was talking to. Then he left the room when I got off the phone and tried to debate with me. I told him I'm not going through another year with this behavior. I also said, "if you don't stay in school, I told him he would have to leave". After I told him that he then said he was going to go to school, Thank God! When he came home that afternoon, he asked me how I felt and also apologized again.

The next day he had a therapy appointment. I took him when he got in that day from school. Now don't get me wrong, I know he's been under stress at school and this new school is a little academically harder, so he really has to stay focused. I know that Xman is capable of making good grades, he's no dummy, he just gets a little too laxed and as a parent, I've got to keep him on task. I don't want him to get in a slump. As a parent, that's my job. Anyway, I took him to therapy that lasted about 45 minutes. I spoke to the therapist after the session was up. He told me that it was a good session and Xman did well. I also asked him about the paper that he fills out before Xman goes in to see therapist that explains how he's feeling, whether it be depressed,

Thanksgiving Holiday

suicidal, etc. The doctor said actually it was not that bad at all, seems like some progress was made. Amen!

CHAPTER 17:

The Nativity Story

This was Christmas vacation and I'm filled with joy unspeakable. Xman's last day was yesterday, and it was a half day. I got a tree and decorated it. I got some of my gifts already, I'm expecting some family. This is my favorite time of year. I feel it should be a big celebration of lights, to celebrate the Lord of Lords, the King of Kings into the world. The miraculous birth of Christ. Jesus was born in a manger, who cares if we don't know the exact day of his birth. If we can celebrate our birthday and we haven't done nowhere near what He did for us, we surely can celebrate The Creator's birth. Make a day for it, take time to praise Him for what all he did. The love he has for us, no one can match, period!

Yesterday was Sunday, we went to church. That morning Xman and I were debating on what church to go to. I wanted to go to our old church that we are members of, and he wanted to go to the new one. We had been 2 times before, and Xman says he really likes it. Xman told me about something that I didn't know that happened to him at the old church. I took all this in consideration, so we ended up going to the new one. I was praying to myself that morning for Xman to see why we celebrate Christmas, because he was saying that it's a pagan holiday. I told him the real reason why we celebrate is because of Jesus' birth, and the miracle virgin conception, but I couldn't find a way to explain it, so that he could truly understand. I knew in the past that the old church never really explained it, so he never understood. Xman just saw all the glitz and glamor, he had never been told the Christmas story about Jesus. I should have read it to him myself. I don't know where my head was at the time. I really didn't think he would understand. I kept going to the old church, but they never did read about the Nativity. That really bothered me a lot, because people need to know the truth. When we got to the new church everyone was so nice. I spoke to the pastor's wife for quite a while then, the pastor came up to the front and started to preach. He spoke about Mary in the Bible, and how favored Mary was to have God's child. Then they had a worship service with music and praise. After the worship they put on a movie, and it started out with Mary sitting on some stone, and then I knew my son was getting ready to see why, and how we celebrate. I was so elated with joy I almost started to cry; this had never happened before. It was beautiful plus, Xman started worshipping himself, and singing the songs which he didn't do at the other church anymore. He also told me that he felt the other church was too worldly. When they had the altar call, we went up for prayer, even though we had already received Jesus, we needed prayer for other things. The pastor brought out anointing oil and anointed our heads and prayed over us in tongues. That also never happened to us at the other church. Now this is a smaller group at this new church, but they are on fire for the Lord. It doesn't matter how big the congregation is because like the Bible says, if there are 2 or more, I am in the midst of you. That's what the Lord said in His Word, Matthew 18:19, Amen! When we were leaving, I had had only four dollars on me, and Xman and I divided it to put it in for the offering. I wanted to give something even though I wish I would have had more to put in, this was at the offering time. Then, pastor released the church, and his wife told us to get a snack if we wanted. I saw some cake there and we went for that. As we were leaving, a lady came up to me and said that she wanted to give me something, and she put $10.00 in my hand, I didn't have any money, so I thanked her for it, and received it as a blessing. When we got home, we just chilled, the whole day was at peace.

CHAPTER 18:

Out of Control, give it to God!

Over the Christmas Vacation, Xman and I had got into yet another altercation over my phone. It was ringing, I was washing dishes while we were both in the kitchen. My hands were wet, and he was by my phone, I said out loud "I'm not going to answer it" but I did walk over to see the number. As I walked over, Xman had the phone in his hand, I thought he was about to either answer it, and possibly say something foul to the person on the line or hang up on them. I didn't know for sure, so I panicked because he has spontaneously done that before therefore, I didn't know what to expect. I tried to get the phone from him as I was telling him to please not say anything to who's on the line. I was also praying that he wouldn't throw it at the same time. We ended up fighting over the phone and it ended up him slapping me real hard in my face to the point that my eye glass lens fell out. I was shocked and angered and hurt. All I could do was cry and want to hit him back, but that would have got me out of a parent's character. If I would have hit him back, and not used my brain, to think of what might have happened to me, because my son is big and strong and doesn't know his own strength. That would have been dumb! I didn't want to tell anyone right away and I was really hesitant on calling 911, because I didn't know how this could unfold. I was just thinking to myself this could become tragic. As I was screaming at him "you hit me", he started apologizing again for the millionth time. I was so tired of some of the same. He started saying "I want to kill myself" and "do you forgive me mom". I was still holding my face in disbelief that that was my reality. He kept saying "go ahead and call 911 so that they can

911, Broken. Give it to God!

come and shoot me". I was lost for words and so hurt. We finally spoke about what had just happened and I told him he better calm down and to take his medicine which was a sedative, or I will call 911. I was at the end of my rope. I also ended up taking a sedative myself, my nerves were out of control, and I didn't know the outcome this would take. I had forgot all about the prayer line because I was so thrown off, see that's how the devil works, he always tries to throw you off, I bit in this time. I have to stay focused. I was scared at the same time and feared for my life and his also. He finally went out of the room, and I went out also to my room. All of a sudden, I could hear him screaming "Mom, I just want to kill myself". Then he asked me to call the prayer line and I did. He got on the phone with them, and I felt a glimpse of hope as he was on the phone. I started praying to myself for help. Xman was on the prayer line for quite a while. Then he came into where I was and shoved the phone in my hand and said that the guy on the phone line was slow. I took the phone and prayed with that same guy on it and when I hung up, things started to simmer down a little bit but, right after I hung up Xman said he was going to call the Suicide Hotline, and he did. Up to this point, I hadn't told anyone, not even his father. I thought to myself, if I tell his father, he will probably come over and take the new phone he had just bought Xman and he wouldn't give it back to him at all. I knew that my son needed his phone in case of an emergency, so I didn't want to do that. I was at an all-time loss, we finally ended up after several apologies, both of us, going to our room and falling asleep. Thank God! He went in his room. He had already taken the meds and so had I, and I thanked the Lord and went to sleep. Sometimes I believe you should consider medicine if you're not working with a normal circumstance, such as we had. This circumstance brought on very high anxiety, don't get me wrong, I don't want to get dependent on drugs. They make different meds for different things, and this was a time to use them.

The next day his father came by, because the night before Xman had told his father to shut up, and his father and I weren't raised like that, to talk to your parents with no respect, or consequences. When he came, I had told him that Xman had slapped me in my face, and I was going to call

911. When his dad heard this, he told Xman to hit him if he wants to bully someone and see how that turns out for you. I really wasn't going to tell his father, but I knew he needed to be disciplined. Xman started explaining and lying about what happened. We had a very long discussion on that incident, which ended up with Xman having to give up his new phone until he started respecting us and meaning his apologies for his actions. I knew this would happen about his phone, but he had to grow in this area. We both agreed to it as his parents, that's best. You know that this was one of the best ways to get his attention, that was by taking away something he likes, like electronics or his phone. Xman was very upset, you could tell he was convicted of what he had done.

Well, the Christmas holiday is winding on down. Xman and I started bonding more since the phone situation. He has been coming out of the room, more helping with chores and also responding to me a lot better, don't get me wrong, we still have a way to go but we're making progress. Thank you, Jesus! When we get in a heated argument, my anxiety level goes up fast, because I don't know what to expect. That's why I have to stay in prayer. Well enough of that, I will leave it in God's hands and move on. I also thought this Christmas I would have a chance to see my grandkids, but they live in Southern California. We live where when you come to see us, you have to go through what we call the "Grapevine", and it goes up 4,400 ft. and sometimes in the winter, they shut it down due to bad weather like ice or snow or other various conditions. This time it was shut down a lot during their vacation. I really miss the family, my mother, my father, my brother, my daughter, and grandkids, and also my friends. I know it's a time for everything, it says it in the Bible. I believe the Lord will make a way for me to see them soon.

Xman is going back to school today, this is his first day back. I've been in prayer for the rest of this year. I also gave a First Fruit Offering, and I've been doing that every year since I found out about it. I found out how much of a blessing you receive and believe me, I have been so blessed. My Lord has provided me with a home that I bought, I've been in it for three years now, also, new furniture. I didn't like the linoleum on the floors, and the Lord found someone that could do my bathrooms and kitchen with brand new stone floors for a little bit of nothing. They look awesome, also, all new appliances that I just paid off in full, and a support team in school for my son. Now you can't tell me I don't serve an awesome God! I expect my son to graduate on time and continue going to school and possibly get a degree. God has plans for me and my family. I've got court coming up for the case with Xman at his old school for neglect, and bullying abuse. I thought I found an attorney, but it seems like no one wants to take on this kid's case especially on a contingency. I'm still looking for counsel. I had gone to a place where they could find you an attorney, still no help. Court is just a week away. I need a miracle for this. By the way, Xman had a pretty good day yesterday for his first day of school, amen!

I spoke to his counselor yesterday and he told me that he was dropping Xman's Health class, because he didn't need it anymore. That was good for Xman, then he only needed to focus on his other academics more and bring up his grades in those classes. I received his report card over his vacation, and it was a little better than the last one and also, a couple of teachers said he was improving since our I.E.P. meeting so, we still have hope. Pretty soon I'm going to need to get with his dad and go graduation shopping for his cap and gown, and ring. Today's a new day, it rained yesterday and where we live in the Central Valley of California, we need it bad for the produce, and we also live in a grapevine territory, it's beautiful, lots of different colored trees, like all gold, and all burgundy trees that I've seen living here. I originally grew up in Southern California where it didn't take but a minute to get to the beach, but we moved to a slower territory due to my circumstance, and for my kid's sake. Plus, the cost of living is a lot less expensive here and you get a lot for your money, and like I say, it's beautiful here, it has four seasons, gorgeous with mature landscaping. Here you can drop a seed anywhere, of almost anything, and it will grow. By the way, I gave Xman his phone back from punishment over the incident we had. It's also the Bible Belt of California, the land is blessed.

Yesterday it really rained. My son walked home from school in it. He had called me to pick him up, but I was across town, and he didn't want to wait. I got home about an hour after him and he was there waiting for

Out of Control, give it to God!

me to come in. When I was driving home, I could barely see, the windows were starting to fog, and it was pouring down. I prayed my way home. Like I said before, we really need the rain here for our crops and I also love the rain too, it makes you want to get cozy. Xman seems to have been in good spirits when I came in until later on that evening before bed, he started to mention a teacher from school and also after, he had spoken to his sister on the phone. I don't know what they talked about, but I do know that earlier I had phoned my mother's house where she lives, my daughter answered, and rushed me off the phone due to her wanting to speak with my mother about her day, my daughter's day. I figured that my daughter must have had some issues with her day by the tone of her voice. I told her to go ahead so she could vent to my mother, sometimes it's with me, or sometimes with my mom. Xman also spoke to her, and it seemed like a little hostility rubbed off on him too. I said to myself, here we go. He started to act defiant, and I told him I wasn't for all this tonight. I told him to calm down or I was going to call his father and also take away his phone. He went back in his room, and I did call his father, but his father said he wasn't feeling well, and he had to take some medicine, and was going to bed. Xman finally went in his room, and I went in mine and went to bed too. The next day was Friday, and we had a 3-day

weekend coming up for Martin Luther King's Day, and we have an appointment with a psychiatrist this morning.

CHAPTER 19:

Side Effects with Meds

Today is Tuesday, the day after MLK holiday, and also his doctor's appointment. When we were on our way to the appointment, Xman was very frustrated, he didn't want to go. He kept saying things like, "I'm tired, I want to go back home", I told him we can't go back, I already cancelled one appointment, and this is the rescheduled one and we can't miss it, or they'll drop you. Now when we arrived there, no one was there yet, we were going to be the first appointment. My son didn't want to fill out the info, so I filled it out for him. When they opened up the office, I asked if the doctor was in yet and the receptionist told me that he'd be in at any time now. After about 10 minutes, I saw the doctor standing at the window of the receptionist's desk speaking to her. I was glad he had come in on time, we were about 20 minutes early anyway. The doctor then called Xman in. He opened the door and I saw the doctor really good, he was casually dressed, nice, with silver hair, tall, of Indian descent with a deep voice. I was trying to gesture to him that I needed to speak to him before Xman went in, but Xman rushed in. Then I spoke out to the doctor, and told him that I would speak to him after the session's over. After about 10-15 minutes, Xman came out and said, "the doctor wants to see you mom". I went in and sat down, and he started going over the medication he had given us at the first visit, and I told the doctor Xman really didn't take it and the doctor looked a little bothered by it. It felt to me like that's all it was about, was the meds to this doctor. I don't know if the doctor forgot, but when I found out what the side effects were that he told me, I really didn't want my son to take the drugs at all. To be honest, to

105

me, these doctors are using these kids and teens as lab rats to test the meds and see what side effects come out of these drugs. I had told the doctor the last time we were here that the side effects were terrible. The doctor had told me one of them could cause tremors and your eyes could roll back in your head, and another one could cause my son to grow breasts. I was at the end of my rope with it plus, half of the drugs weren't approved by the FDA. The doctor still prescribed the meds, and never had any conversation with Xman about really anything or how he was doing etc. It was all about giving meds. As I walked back out to the waiting room, there sat my son, and the room was full of patients. I felt so discouraged, also, before I left the doctor told me he wanted my son to take more labs. I had remembered the first time we went; he sent us to get labs and I told him we already had them, and he asked me where we went. He didn't even have a record of them.

This weekend we missed church, I was getting over a bad cough and cold I had had for two weeks. I was drained mentally and physically, so we ended up watching church on TV. I finally got my check and paid my bills and my First Fruit Offering for the year. The First Fruit, if I haven't' already explained, are what you give to the Lord in finances, your best every first of the year because, I was told and read, from all first of your increase goes to the Lord out of any of your finances earned, especially at the beginning, that determines how your year will go, and so far, since I've been doing it, I've been very blessed. In Matthew 6, it tells us first things first. I also went to court last week for my hearing regarding Xman's case and the judge granted me more time to get my case together and find representation, I was real happy about that.

Yesterday my son brought home his report card and I was also happy to see that he had brought up his grades. He had A+'s but the other grades weren't put in yet so I'm just waiting on them, but so far so good. I called his counselor and left a message to see if they knew what the other grades are. I also called his dad and spoke to him about going to pick out his ring for graduation, and like I said before, when you buy the ring, the cap and gown come with it for free, so that saves us some money to do something else for his graduation. I love a good deal, don't you? I also plan for some of

Side Effects with Meds

the family that can make it to come up and celebrate with us. It has been a long haul and we can all go out to eat and take a load off. I can't wait, it's as if I was the one graduating. I'm so proud of my son I could cry just thinking about it. He's really been working hard, and we've been interacting more. He's coming out of his room more and his confidence is higher.

CHAPTER 20:

Rose Bowl & Cable Company Issues

This weekend we went to our new church, and it was so spiritually fulfilling. The message was in Jeremiah 29:11-13, which says, "for I know the thought that I think towards you says the Lord, thought of peace, and not evil, to give you a future and a hope. Then you will call upon me and go pray to me and I will listen to you". Also in James 4:7-8 it says, "therefore submit to God, resist the devil, and he will flee from you. Draw near to God and He will draw near to you". It was so awesome, the Pastor gave us several examples of the message, people were speaking in tongues, seems like the Holy Spirit fell on almost everyone in the room, if not everyone, some people were crying even. It was a relief, burdens were lifted. It felt like I was at a revival, we all held hands and prayed. It was amazing. I felt brand new! Even my son was praying and singing. It was a miracle! After the service, we went out to lunch. We were talking about some of everything. I told him I am so proud of him.

This is a new week, I started it off by prayer and asking the Lord to give us focus, favor, peace and to break off any bondages, also that any assignment of the enemy be cancelled. It went pretty smooth. I had got a little depressed thinking about how far away I am from my family, and how many memories I could be making with them if I was closer. I spoke to the Lord about it, and I called my mother at the end of the week. My mother told me that my brother told her that if she wanted to, she could move in with him. My mother lives in Pasadena, California. It's so pretty there, the trees make the city so quaint, there are a lot of older, well-made homes there. They're also

911, Broken. **Give it to God!**

building a lot of new ones too. A lot of the riff raff that used to be in certain areas in the city couldn't afford it, so most of them moved away. Don't get me wrong, we have bad and good in all areas, sometimes you can't avoid it, that doesn't mean you have to have money either, but there were a lot of druggies coming from some of the less fortunate areas of Pasadena that were causing a lot of problems, such as, theft, etc. Pasadena also, once a year during the New Year, has the Rose Parade there, where they make the Floats out of beautiful roses and other flowers and materials. People come from everywhere in the world to see it, a lot of schools get involved, their bands, and cheerleaders, and the different Grand Marshals. You can also see beautiful horses in it, music, singers, etc. They have the football game after it at the Rose Bowl. The best two teams played each other that won for the season. It's a packed affair, you can't even get through the city if you're not already there. People even camp out over night for it, it's real nice.

I joined the new church, Xman and I have been going to, I really like it. They called us both up after the sermon, which was about pornography, and how it affects lives and breaks up homes, and how many churches don't talk about it when they need to because it has a big effect on teens, husbands, wives, and it needs to be addressed. It's an addiction like drugs, and the statistics are overwhelming. Everyone needs to know about these sensitive, real issues because people are dying and go to hell behind them. We need to stop sugar coating these issues. The Lord is so awesome! It even says in His Word that all good things come from above and that His Word doesn't come back void. Tithings and offerings are key as well.

I went to see a new attorney and gave his assistant my paperwork to scan for the case yesterday, and I also went to my tax guy to do my taxes this week. Everything seems to be going pretty good so far. The only thing that happened was at the beginning of the week, an incident with the cable company I go through, seems like the devil started to work through one of the supervisors there. I call up to pay my bill and I had told them to read the notes because the bill was wrong and too high, over a hundred and some odd dollars more than it should have been, so I was disgusted. The person I was speaking with had put me on hold forever, and I told her I don't want

Rose Bowl & Cable Company Issues

to be on hold for a long time, because I have things to do and other bills to pay. Then she wanted to transfer me all over the place to different people to help with it because I guess she felt I should still pay the bill no matter what amount it was, and no matter what I told her didn't matter either. The problem with the bill was that not only was it too high, it was that they weren't reading all the notes involved with it. I was told by two other customer service people that the bill before was going to be less, because I had paid for it on my credit card at the time. I called in last month because I had to have them come out and install a wall unit that I had already purchased myself. The bill was only for the install not their bracket that was put in, because I was using my own bracket I had already bought elsewhere. When I called the cable company, I told them that and they said since I'm using my own bracket, they would only charge me $50.00 dollars for install, but when I called back and heard on the automated service the payment info said I owed $267.00, I hit the roof. I kept being transferred around to different people and then I got supposedly the main supervisor, an arrogant, cocky guy that told me not only did I have to pay everything the bill said, but that now I was on a new contract, and I couldn't get out of it. I lost it! The next day a lady by the name of Goodman I believe, she was Jewish, called me back and resolved the whole issue. The lady was from their corporate office and boy was that a relief, she went over everything and had read my notes, she sounded real young but very sharp, she told me that she saw where I had paid on my card the $50.00 and deducted the bill by over $240.00 and some odd dollars, leaving me a balance of only $21.00 and some change for that month, also reduced my bill, and took me off contract. I was so impressed with her customer service skills. I didn't know what to say. I got her direct phone number line, and the corporate address to write them a letter on her behalf, and to let them know how much of an asset she is to their company. We truly need more people like her in high places of authority to help us. That's honest and fair, she went over and above for me, and for that I am truly thankful. She kept me with the cable company, believe me. Thank God for her! If it wasn't for her, I was going to cancel, and call the BBB (known as the Better Business Bureau), and possibly file a formal complaint, and then,

911, Broken. **Give it to God!**

tell everyone I know dealing with this company, about the misrepresentation on their part.

This week my son had another blow up. President's Day was coming up on Monday, that Sunday I had found a barber shop open to get his hair cut because he was wearing dreads, and I don't think he was washing them well. They started to smell real bad like mildew, so his dad and I told him we were going to get his hair done different, so it would be easier to take care of. His dad's girlfriend came over that weekend on Saturday and cut out the dreads, and washed his hair and conditioned it. The next day I took him to Super Cuts, and they cut off his ends and evened it out. That next Monday was President's Day and back to school on Tuesday, but he had a doctor's appointment with his psychiatrist Dr. B., and I had told him about it the night before, so he knew. I woke him up, told him to get ready, and that night before, I had seen a mouse in our garage when I was out there that ran up the pole, into the ceiling towards the attic. I ran in the house, locked the door leading to the garage, and I had a flip flop that I took off that was holding the door open. The tumbler on the knob of the door was messed up, and if you shut the door all the way, the door would lock on you, and you couldn't get it back open. That's why the flip flop was holding it. I went to go out the garage to start the car up that morning so we could get ready to go see Xman's doctor. I couldn't seem to get the door open, before I had been using a knife and that would open it but this time it didn't. The clock was ticking, and we were running late. Xman started yelling at me to open the door of the garage, and I kept telling him to go in his room and start getting dressed. Then he threw a large basket at me that was filled with junk on top of the kitchen counter and all that junk went everywhere, all over the kitchen. I was sweating, and panicking trying to open this door to get in the garage, and get to my car, so we could leave. He kept antagonizing me and we were yelling back and forth. I told him I was going to call his father or 911 if he didn't stop. I picked the phone up, called his dad because he wouldn't stop, his father was asking me what was going on, I told him and asked him to please talk to Xman. I gave him my phone, he snatched it out of my hand and told his father that he wasn't doing anything wrong, then I

112

Rose Bowl & Cable Company Issues

told Xman to give me back the phone and call his father on his phone, he threw it at me, and it hit me in my face so hard that the phone broke open. This, I mind you, happened real fast, the problem escalated quick. I also tried to protect myself by blocking his hits and swinging back at him too. The night before I had been drinking and medicating heavily over issues going on in our home, like our finances for instance that I receive, mostly about my paycheck that I got to pay our bills, because of so much confusion that had been stirred up in the house, I forgot to fill out my hours and the President's Day holiday was that Monday. I knew I had forgot to put in the hours for payment, and it was going to make my paycheck late. I knew I had to call up the IHSS office, that stands for In-Home Supportive Services. I report my hours biweekly, and I had forgot and my check this time was going to be late due to all the drama, at least an extra week and I really couldn't afford to be late because all the bills were due, most of them at the beginning of the month, like my mortgage etc. Being a single mom is not easy especially in my circumstance, also living in your own home, taking care of a teenage son going through puberty, and Autism and other issues. I was beside myself and found myself medicating. I was contemplating calling the police. I was worried something could happen to my son if I called the police, but I need to because this could go bad quick. I was a little afraid to call because of all the stories you hear on the news, so I told my son to call his father also to pick him up and leave, but then I remembered that I had put our situation on the prayer line list as well. I previously called several times before about Xman and told them our problems. They had been praying for us. My emotions started to alter, and my faith kicked in and a small voice in my head told me that everything was going to be alright, my fear subsided, and a sense of peace came over me.

I just bought a new car, a Range Rover, one of my favorite cars. God blessed me that day with it. Everything went smooth through their financing department, my credit score was on point, and at an all-time high, and you know it takes good credit and you need to be on time with bill payments. Don't forget your taxes on your home, and to include them in your house payment monthly. Try to get your interest rate low as well, make it an all-in-one payment so you won't have to hustle up taxes twice a year. I took a real estate course and passed principal 101, but didn't take the state exam, long story. For your FYI, never let anything distract you.

CHAPTER 21:

Life Skills Teacher & Blow Ups

The next week everything went a lot better, my son and I were bonding better, he was telling me about school and a teacher he was having problems with that I had to reach out to, and call that teacher up, and ask her what was going on, because in all but one other class, he was getting great grades. As a matter of fact, mostly A+'s, and I needed to see what and why his teacher was failing him, when he had no missing assignments when I checked his portal that gives you all his grades on the computer. So, I spoke with the teacher, and she told me about a test he took and said that Xman missed 9 out of 14 questions. Now let me remind you that when we had our last I.E.P., it was written in it that he could retake any test if he scored low, and I also told her that at least he's putting up an effort. Then she told me that there was an assignment that I needed to help him to complete, that's all she needed to see, that it had been submitted over the computer on my part, and that would help his grade also. So, I spoke to him when he got in from school and he told me he knew what she was talking about, and I told him I wanted to do my part. I needed no more on my plate. The rest of the weekend went so-so, after him going to church, it helped a lot, it brought a sense of peace over us, but I knew we still needed to deal with that project for his class. That we both had to finish our parts on that assignment.

This was a new week, and it started off me having to call his counselors and that teacher that needed us to do the project for filling out the application online for the college funding. Xman will be needing that, it had got out of hand. Every time we tried to do it on his computer, it would either

911, Broken. Give it to God!

say error or the computer would lock up on us so that we couldn't complete the assignment. I was at the end of my rope with this. I called the prayer line to get help. I finally spoke to his teacher, Mrs. L., and set up an appointment with her, to come into the school for that class that needed the computer work from the both of us turned in, which was his transitional class. This class teaches you life skills and prepares you for the outside world. When I got to the school I checked in with the front desk. I was a little early, so I went outside, and made a phone call to my mother in Pasadena, California. I told her why I was at the school, of course she already knew the deal. I went back inside and started walking towards his class, and as I was walking to Xman's class, I heard a loud buzzing sound and bells going off, wouldn't you know it was a fire drill happening. I thought I was going to lose it. Here comes all the students running out of class to go to the field and wait till it's over. I saw Xman's teacher Mrs. L., and she told me I could follow them to the field, but I couldn't that day. I was wearing very high heels so, what I did instead of walking to the field, was sat down on top of a small concrete wall and waited for them to come back to class. I'd say it took around 15 minutes before they came back. When I saw them walking back, I just went on back to Xman's classroom and waited on the teacher. When everyone got settled in, Mrs. L. his teacher, called Xman's gym teacher and sent Xman to the gym. We finally proceeded to start working on the computer for finishing up the job for his project. Xman's info was already in, I just had to redo mine. We even had to make up a new Gmail account just to get into the program because I couldn't get it on their computer for some strange reason, so Xman had to make me up a Gmail account. I finally got the program, and we finished it up. It really worked my patience to say the least, and everyone else's too. It started to get very tedious for us, but God is good! It got done and literally we all jumped for joy, and I even did a little dance. We all hugged one another, and I left to go home. Take note that when I first got to the school that morning, I was in a set it off mood, because of having so much trouble doing this program, but when I left, the Lord humbled my heart. Thank you, Lord!

Life Skills Teacher & Blow Ups

Now it was the weekend and Xman had a bit of an attitude because I couldn't find his Dr. Dre Beats Box, it got out of hand again. I remembered that I took it from him for being disrespectful and I put it up in a closet but, one of my acquaintance's brothers came by not too long ago and he knew I was tired. I fell asleep while he was there, and I thought he stole it out of my closet. I fell asleep on accident believe me. I had been mentally and physically drained and had taken some meds, that was all it took, and I was out. I didn't want to tell my son that I even thought the guy stole it, but when my son asked me for it, I knew what I thought was true had happened, because this person had stolen from me before. I was assuming that he did it again. This same guy stole my car keys and took my car. I had to call his aunt and she then called his mother, it just so happened that he was just walking into his mother's house when they were on the phone and his mother told him to bring me back my car, and he did, thank God! I didn't even know that the Bluetooth was missing, yet at the same time, I started checking around the closet and couldn't find it. I just thought right then, it was him that took it because no one else had been over recently that would do that. Don't get me wrong, the sad part about this is I always had people stealing from me. I was so hurt, because I knew my son would find out about it. I'd have to explain to him, and I knew this would be a trigger. I was crushed and was also mad at myself. When my son asked, at first, I told him I had misplaced it, I didn't need him to flare up. He called his father, his father got all upset he threatened me. I told Xman I was going to call 911 on him if he started to get crazy. It was a mess, my son then started to go off and it all went downhill from there. I told him I would buy him another one as soon as I got paid and replace it. Now that weekend we did make it to church and that was good, it brought back peace in our home.

That next Monday, my son went on to school however, I did medicate myself a couple of days through that next week, because my son did occasionally bring up the music box, and we did have some arguments throughout that week again about it. I felt really bad about the whole thing, then I got to a point where I fell to my knees, and told the Lord I need help from all this self-medicating. I was at the end of my rope. I was crying and very depressed.

911, Broken. **Give it to God!**

I had spoken to my boyfriend that lived in L.A. and told him I was going to start going to Bible Study to get started getting sober, he had been pretty worried about me because he knew about the drug use and wanted me clean. I was disgusted with myself and getting high was just making things worst. My boyfriend also had been going to AA classes and church himself and would always sound so happy and cheerful. He would sometimes explain to me some of the things he experienced when going, and it helped listening to him, to realize I needed some help, especially from the Lord to get straight. I cried out and He heard my prayers, thank you Lord Jesus!

CHAPTER 22:

Covid & the Key in The Bible Box

That Wednesday, the news was on that morning, and it was speaking about that new virus everyone was worried about. The Corona virus, and how many people were infected, and what States it was in. They also said there was one person in my city that was quarantined in their home. That Wednesday I contacted my pastor, and he called me back and told me that we would be having Bible Study that night at church at 7pm. I also called the NA, and asked about some meetings to go to and got the addresses, I found a couple to go to by my house. I made it to Bible Study and boy did I need that. We started out with praise and worship, and everyone there put their hearts into it. You could feel the love and Holy Spirit in the room. The message that night was about tithing and offering, a few people read, I didn't get a chance to because it wasn't enough time left. We also prayed at the end of the study for all our loved ones, also about the Corona Virus, it was great. I felt so much better and at peace. I came home, the house was good, and I went to sleep like a baby.

My son Xman is now on Spring Break, and I got a message from his school that because of the virus, their break would be extended for at least an extra 2-3 weeks more. Now Friday was my son's last day of school. He told me he wanted to go to the mall that coming Saturday. I told him that's O.K.

Now Sunday, I made it to church, I also felt the urge to go as I told you that Wednesday evening for Bible Study. I ran to God's house, and that's where I needed to be. The next Sunday, I also made it again to church, Amen! I went by myself to church, I let Xman stay home but before I left, we both had breakfast and we watched one of my favorite ministers on TV together. He spoke of an incident that happened with a father and son. The boy asked his father "if I get all A's for graduating from college, would you buy me a car?" His father told him maybe, so they went to look at cars and the son picked out a beautiful sports car. His father did like it. When the boy graduated from college, he went to his father to show him his grades and his father handed him a small box. The boy opened it and was disappointed because he saw that the box was small, and he was expecting to see a car. Inside the box was a Bible, he pushed the box back to his father and left mad at his dad. He didn't speak to his dad for years however, he went on, got married, later his wife had a son and he wanted to show his father his new baby grandson. He remembered all the memories about how him, and his dad were when he was growing up. His heart started softening up and he told his wife that they were going to drive across state to go see his dad. When he got there, he found out that his father had died. He was so hurt and felt so bad that he had stayed mad at him for so long. He went to the office of his father's and saw the same box that the Bible was in. He opened up the box, and there was that same Bible. This time he opened up the Bible and a key fell out; it looked like a car key. He went to the garage and to his surprise, there sat that same sports car he saw years ago when they had gone to that car lot. All this time the car that he picked out was in the garage. If he had only opened up the Bible and saw the key, he would have known that his father hadn't forgot about him and got him that sports car he wanted years ago. This was a true story, goes to show you that sometimes we let the devil deceive us into thinking the worst instead of God's best, and let our focus get thrown off. The son also missed all those years being mad and missed all that time with his father. He could have been driving the car as well. If he would have only opened the Bible and gave his father a chance. The moral of the story to me is life is too short for unforgiveness and pettiness. Both my son and I listened to that true story together, I just pray my son got something out of it.

Now the next time we were to go to church was Wednesday for Bible Study, but I got a call from our pastor's wife stating that, because of the virus,

Covid & the Key in The Bible Box

they would no longer have church or Bible Study at the facility we had been going to but, we were welcome to join in over the phone or Facebook. It has killed quite a number of people; it has spread to different parts of the world now, and it's now a pandemic. Italy and parts of New York have it really bad right now. Last count here was around 3 people who died where I'm at. When they find out you have it, they keep you in quarantine. The symptoms are a dry cough and fever. I've been in prayer for all my loved ones, Israel and others, it's no joke. All these things had been mentioned in the book of Matthew 24th chapter. That whole chapter tells of the signs of the end, the Lord tells His disciples.

Passover is coming up and I've notified a lot of my people about the Passover Offering, because I know that we as Christians, should participate in it, even if we're not Jewish, because we can bless them and at the same time, we can receive a blessing. We need to bless and honor the Jewish High Holy Holidays because it also says in Genesis 12:3, "I will bless those who bless you (meaning Israel and its people) and I will curse those who curse you and in you all the families of the earth shall be blessed". I truly believe it. It has blessed me and mine very much. We might have issues, but the Lord always works out our problems and answers my prayers. Just like today, my son had been having difficulties getting online. Last Friday, his father and his father's girlfriend stayed on the phone with him for over 4 hours and still couldn't get him online. Everyone was burnt out; we had been back and forth talking to his school with different staff and teachers, but nothing helped. It caused myself and son to argue in the home, I would leave the house just to give us some space so that we wouldn't start fighting over and over due to no school because of their break and the virus. The school started sending us texts and phone messages that the students would have to go online and do their assignments. All hell broke loose over the weekend, so I left. I called the prayer line on Monday morning for the new week and told them what had been happening in our home. Right after I called, I received info that they would be getting in touch with my son to help. I was so overwhelmed. I went back to medicating. I thank the Lord that Monday when we went up to the school that there were about five ladies with packets for his classes, and they gave them to us. Then when we got home my son seemed relieved as well, and he got a call from the school that helped him to get online, and he started his packets today. The Lord once again heard my cry and stepped in and handled it. Thank you, Jesus!

Over the weekend my car wouldn't go into reverse. My son had told me that Friday that he never went online and that he was only filling out the packets and we ended up in another argument. I left, but before I left, I called the school and told them that he never went online. I was so upset. The school also told me because of the Covid virus, they would be shutting down for the rest of the year, and maybe in June they might reopen, but that was a big if. I was worried that my son wouldn't be able to hand in his packets and get credit for doing them so that he could get his final grades and get his certificate. I also received a letter in the mail about his financial aid funding, that said he had to fill the forms out if he wanted his funding. It also mentioned drafting, like military, and if you weren't in a mental facility that he could possibly be drafted. There was an 800 number to call. I called it and told them that my son had Autism, then they told me it still needed to be filled out, signed and returned. I had my son sign and date it; I will be mailing that today. This is getting deep, like my son's father would say "this is deeper than the ocean". I also had the handy man that put my brakes on come over to look at the car. I told him I had to have my car towed from where it was because it wouldn't go into reverse. He came over, told me that I could still drive it for a while until I could get it fixed, just not to put it in a place where I would have to reverse. I went to the store to get a few things because we were running low on food and other supplies. God blessed me there and back safely. You see the Lord did hear my prayer even though my son lied, He still got him his work to do for school, and there would still be a way to contact someone to get him help to go online. When I called back that past Friday, the lady at the school told me she would still be answering the phone for the school if I needed anything, just call her back. I was just upset that my son had lied.

Now this week I was going to AutoZone to buy some oil for the car. I was only a little way from it and my brakes completely locked down. I

Covid & the Key in The Bible Box

couldn't go backward or forward, I was stuck. All I could do was pray. I asked the Lord to just get me into the AutoZone lot, to park off the street until I could get help, and you better believe, that's just what He did. Thank you, Jesus! I could just see the police asking me what I was doing parked in the middle of the street, and believe you me, there were a lot of police patrolling at this time due to the virus. I had to call my insurance company to get a tow and I did just that. The man from AutoZone came out, put the oil in for me and I waited for the tow. About a half hour later, the guy came to tow the car, now due to the virus like I said before, the company wouldn't let anyone ride with the tow truck driver, so I had to call for a ride. I had an acquaintance pick me up and drop me off. They took my car to the shop. The person that was working on my car told me he would call me later after he diagnosed it. When the shop called me back, they told me that the car was ready for pick up. I called for the same acquaintance to take me back to the shop to pick up my car. When I got to the shop, they told me that the bolts on the car where the brakes were supposed to have been fixed, that one fell out and the other bolt was on its way to falling out. That's why it wouldn't reverse or go forward. The guy at the shop also told me that whoever fixed it didn't complete the work. They never tighten them up. He also told me that I could have killed someone or myself if I would have been able to go forward, because if that final bolt would have fallen out, I would have only been able to turn right. Also, if anyone would have been in the way, I would of ran into them not being able to stop. I was so upset but thankful at the time that I took it to the right place to get fixed. Only the Lord gave me the wisdom to take it there, because I had been calling around. Then I called the prayer line and they prayed for me to get it in the right hands, and to give the person wisdom who was fixing it, and for a low price. It all happened in that order. It was also done quickly as well.

Now the weekend coming up was Resurrection Sunday, what the world calls Easter. Of course, no church because of the virus, but we could still watch it on TV, due to all this, Xman wasn't in the best of a mood, so I didn't want to force anything on him. Plus, the Lord doesn't want us to force himself on anyone. I went to the store that morning and got all the things I needed to barbecue and came back. I thought this might break the monotony. Xman didn't want to go with me, it was OK. He stayed home.

New week, Xman told me that he had been feeling depressed, and that I really didn't understand him. I tried to ask him what was bothering him, and he told me that he felt like he didn't have a life. I told him that we have to have hope, God willing, soon this virus shall pass, and you'll be able to get back to normal, meaning checking into college, meeting new friends that are more mature, driving, possibly new hobbies, etc. I just wanted to keep the conversation positive. I need my son on a positive note! I also told him not to isolate so much and come out of the room, take the dog for a walk, walk to the store, or read your driving book. I know things can get tedious because they want us to stay in more due to the virus so that it will slow down the spread of it. A lot of places had been hit hard. Such as New York and Italy, China was the first to get hit. It has killed thousands of people, but I keep on remembering what the Lord said in Matthew Chapter 24, it says all these things will happen before the Lord comes back. We just have to put our trust in God. He's in control. I also thought to myself, this is a wakeup call for us all to return back to The Creator. This has shaken up a lot of things. I've seen on the news, people talking about family more, spending time with their loved ones, creating new ways to occupy their time, also, a lot of things are shut down like malls and small businesses. We have takeout only, no restaurants are open, no parks or movie theaters. You can't be in crowds.

CHAPTER 23:

The Battle

My son told me that he was upset because he won't be able to show his kids, if he has any, any pictures of him on grad night or prom.

Last weekend we had a blow up and he hit the wall and made another hole in it. His dad had to send his girlfriend to pick him up from the Walgreens store. I couldn't handle the tension in the house. This weekend I left on Sunday and stayed out until Monday morning after my son got back from his dad's. I ended up medicating again and getting into two arguments because I was intoxicated. I was still reading The Word and in prayer for my son and I. I knew the Lord will deliver me. I'm not giving up with this battle. I still have hope and faith. After all of that, I thanked God for never leaving me or forsaking me because I knew He was still with me. I had gotten stopped by the police twice and had liquor in the car, but all they asked me was for my I.D. and registration and gave me a pass both times. They didn't see the bottle. The first time I got stopped, the bottle was in my purse, the second time it was under my purse. This is not funny at all; I was seriously sick. It was by the Grace of God that I didn't get taken in for drunk driving. I always came off polite and both times it was trivial matters that I had been stopped for, such as, no front license plate but this particular car and model doesn't have an area in front for plates and the other time, not stopping long enough before turning. I knew it was Jesus that protected me at those times because He knew where my mind was at and allowed them to give me a pass. Plus, I could have lost a lot, especially for my son's sake, he needed me. I'm not trying to make up any excuses for drinking because that was wrong and I knew better, it could have gone real bad, because I was still intoxicated. I had already had four D.U.I.'s, and for those four, I did have to pay a heavy price. I always reminded myself to stay cautious. I wasn't to the point of swerving or noticeable, but obviously my intentions were to get there with the bottle of wine. Thank you, Lord, for saving me from disaster. The next morning, I was home with my son having breakfast and getting a chance to bond more, he had no clue of what happened.

Xman's psychologist and psychiatrist both were due to call him and have either a video chat or phone time with him that week. He was able to speak to both of them and vent which was great being that he had professional help. His psychiatrist wanted him to start taking his prescription of meds every day to see the effect on him. I would have but keep in mind, like before as I have told you, I really didn't want him to take those meds due to the fact that the side effects were worse than the conditions being treated and, no one was going to use my son as a guinea pig.

Now the next week we went to pick up his new packets for him to complete. These were the ones that really mattered as far as him getting graded. There's still another set that I have to pick up when he's finished with these. On the way, there we were, both very frustrated. We were arguing and he even threw my purse into the bushes as he was complaining about having to wait. A young lady by the name of Michelle came out with the packets finally. I was so glad because I was at my wits end waiting too. She pulled up all the teachers on computer that Xman had classes with so that we had all the packets. I was so grateful. Again, with the episode with the purse when Xman threw it, I remembered I had put my necklace in a little pill bottle I had in my purse and I thought it fell out, because I couldn't find it in my purse when I looked. I was so upset and hurt about the whole thing. I didn't feel like cooking after all this, so we went to McDonald's for breakfast and stopped at the store for a few items I needed for home. I looked all over the house when I got home for that pill bottle to see if I had left it behind. I might have put it back in my drawer or something but, I clearly remembered putting it in that bottle and back in my purse. I was going to take it, after I dropped him back off at home, to the man at the post office who had

The Battle

a little booth there to fix jewelry. I had spoken to him while mailing a letter and picking up some stamps. He had written down my phone number to remind me to do so. He had a very kind face, older guy with gray hair, very pleasant attitude. Due to the virus, it was rare to see him in the post office, but I guess the owner that I've seen several times that ran it, offered him a job so that he could make some money during these hard times. A lot of people were laid off. They want social distancing of at least six feet apart from each other. They say it (Covid), stays longer on plastic and counter tops, for 3 days or more, also, they want you to wear a mask, and gloves, if you go out around people. They only allow so many into the markets and other public places at a time. Right now, I received a letter in the mail canceling my court date for Xman against the school district. I rescheduled it two more months down the line. I still haven't received a permanent attorney to handle it and due to this pandemic, who knows when they'll open up the courtrooms or how they'll handle any legal matters. They want everyone to stay at home unless it's an emergency to be out.

I went up to Xman's school today and picked up more packets for his home schooling, ran errands and mailed off Mother's Day cards to my mother, and to my daughter. My daughter and I hadn't been speaking to each other due to a blow up we had about some lies being told to her on Facebook from some haters, that didn't know what they were talking about. I tried to explain to her that all they want to do is divide and destroy her because their own lives are so out of control, and to stop listening to that stuff. We hadn't spoken for over two months, and I was very hurt about it. Then, just yesterday, she text me a long letter. She told me she was tired of me medicating myself but wanted us to get back on track and that she loved me. I text her back and told her that I wanted the same thing too, and that I love her as well. It brought me to tears to hear from her. I had been so isolated I needed that text. In that letter I could tell she came from the heart. I was wrong for some of the things I told her during the time we were feuding, but I was so elated to hear from her, I just wanted to start over. I thought I had lost my one and only daughter. I had been asking about her to my mother that she's living with in Pasadena, Ca., a very quaint and beautiful place where people come from all over just to go to their Rose Parade, and after the parade for the football games. I really missed talking to her. I had been praying and asking the Lord to repair our relationship and you know how great our Lord is, "He" did it!

Now last night was not so good of a night. I was on my way to bed after a long day. I had been praying to the Lord for discernment to let me understand things, and that they would be revealed to me, what was going on in any circumstance I might come across, and it started to happen, it started being revealed. Thank you, Jesus! My son and I got in a really heated fight about him not being able to get his TV program on, and he came raging at my bedroom door, as I was about to go to sleep. He said "mom, open the door", as he was knocking on it very hard. I screamed out "I'm not dressed" and I went to grab my robe, I was just about to lay down, and go to sleep. My air conditioner was broken at the time and that day I'd been on the phone with my "In-home" insurance company for over two hours trying to get them to get someone out to fix it. I was tired. I was already overwhelmed, because the temperature in the house was rising. They told me that the tech couldn't find my home on his GPS, so I would have to reschedule for another day, which would be over three days away at the soonest. I had been hot and miserable all day, then, here comes my son with this TV problem to top it off. Like I said, he was banging on my door to let him in and telling me to take off some of my recordings, because he couldn't get his program on. We ended up arguing and fighting over that. I tried to calm him down, but it only escalated the problem. He started throwing things at me, and cursing. I was at my wits end. Finally, he went in his room and calmed down. I was so stressed. I finally went to sleep. He must have got his TV working; I was so stressed and out of breath. I called his father, he didn't come. All I wanted to do was to go to sleep. I was scared to death and praying that nothing else would happen. I called the prayer line, and finally went to sleep.

This weekend was Mother's Day. I woke up to Xman asking me where we were going to eat for Mother's Day, and I responded to him by saying "I didn't know yet, let me get up first". Then, I remembered that I needed to replace Xman's Bluetooth speaker. I had went to Walmart the other day

The Battle

and bought him a new one, and when he came in that morning, he told me it wasn't working so, I jumped out of bed and told him to get ready to go back to the store and get another one before this gets out of hand, and we could have a possible blow up. I had mentioned it already to him, that I was going to get him one. You know he was not going to let me forget, so as I said, I jumped out of bed, and we went down there and got a replacement for the one I just bought because it wasn't working. He was very anxious and so was I to get this done. We both weren't in the best of a mood at this time even though it was Mother's Day. When we got there it was already hot and crowded, even though it was early in the morning. I also picked up some items for the house and dog food. I was mentally and physically drained. It went pretty smooth in the store, and I was happy about that. I always reminded myself to let the Lord take over at these out-of-control times. When I got home, I started making breakfast and thinking on who I needed to call for Mother's Day. Before I made breakfast, I called my mother and daughter to wish them both a Happy Mother's Day, but my daughter wasn't there. I started texting everyone else that I knew that were mothers, and all my loved ones that I had numbers on. Then Xman and I sat down to eat after making us some breakfast. He started talking about school again and how he didn't want to go back, and I told him he didn't have to, anyway, right now, it was shut down because of the virus. No one knew at this point when the school would reopen. After we ate, I started to clean up the kitchen, remind you, this is still Mother's Day. I did get a lot of texts back from family and loved ones, and I also text my daughter a long note letting her know that I will always love her unconditionally, and if I offended her in any way, I apologize. I also text my love of my life friend to let him know that God had a plan for the both of us. We had been trying to get back together for a long time, but we had a lot of obstacles and distance between us. I just wanted to let him know that I was going to let God work all this out, our getting together, if that's God's Will. I had been praying for a companion, but it seemed like every time we would try to get together, something would interfere with it. I know I needed to resolve some issues that I was dealing with with my son first. I couldn't see how this would work with being in a

911, Broken. Give it to God!

relationship, I was at a dead end. This Mother's Day, all I could do was cry. I was out of it. I started drinking again and medicating. I was sitting on my old couch in the garage and having my own little pity party. I was thinking what's left of my life, now you know that's nothing but the devil putting that in my mind. I continued on thinking about how unhappy and alone I felt in this matter. It seemed like everything was spiraling out of control quick. I was in a dark place, it felt even demonic to say the least. The devil was trying to destroy me. He had me disliking my child, my life. I was having horrific thoughts. I came back in the house, went to my room and as I was walking to my room I looked and saw my son in the kitchen eating, to me at the time he looked like the problem. Thoughts of dislike arose in me. I was thinking of how I could get him out of the home. Thinking maybe putting him in a facility or something, because I started feeling fear of us hurting each other. I was tired of fighting, nothing good came to mind. My mind was racing, I was in fear. There was a battle going on in the mind with the devil and the Lord at the same time. I was a mess. This was what satan wanted, confusion, and I bit into it at the time. Then this feeling came over me, the fear of the Lord surrounded me, I could see it clearly, it was all the meds, and drinking that was causing me to think these thoughts. The devil was using them to help destroy my life and relationships. I thought by medicating, I could numb out my feelings, and not have to think or deal with the problems at hand. All it was doing was putting me into a darker realm of reality that was eventually going to take me out. In an instance I felt a light! A ray of hope coming through as I realized what the Lord was trying to show me, to stop right now, get rid of all the meds and run to Me, I will fight your battle and you will win, so I got rid of the meds or drugs, put down the liquor, started crying out to the Lord for help. I ran out the house to my car in the garage, got into it, opened the garage door, backed the car out, looked around myself, started looking up at the sun, and it was so bright and big, brighter than I have ever seen it. I started getting a feeling of relief. I started crying and thanking God, because I was feeling the deliverance and surrendering feeling that the Lord had not left me or forsaken me. He let me know He was still in control of my life, and it was going to be OK. In the Bible, it

The Battle

states that the devil comes to kill, steal and destroy, but God gives us life. I thank the Lord for that, because I thought I was doomed to darkness and death. Now I received comfort from the Lord and hope again. Like I said, I got delivered instantly from meds and drinking, I had no desire afterwards for anything at all. It took the Lord to shake things up for this to happen. He let me know, in order to progress, to have a better way of life, and to be able to have a clear understanding of what's going on with my son, I needed to be convicted and corrected. We all do.

CHAPTER 24:

The Graduation

Now at last we were informed, Xman's graduation was coming up, now because of the virus and social distancing, they were doing things a little differently. I was notified that Xman had an appointment time to be there. We were to drop him off in the parking lot on one side of the school, then we were to go around to the other parking lot and watch him cross the stage, get his certificate, take pictures and be videotaped. After that, he was to meet us at the car, and we immediately take off. No crowds, or hand shaking, or hugs. Xman was very disappointed in this, and so were we. It wasn't traditional at all. It didn't even seem like a graduation. I had picked up his cap and gown that week, I also had to run out real quick and pick him up some dress slacks, shirt and shoes. I was limited to the places I could go, because all the places I wanted to go to, like Macy's, or other nice places, were shut down due to the virus. I believe they had curbside orders, but they would have had to have been ordered way in advance. I only had two days to make it happen. Everything was a big rush. The day of the graduation, I did his hair early that morning so that it would look fresh. As I was washing it in the kitchen sink, some water squirted on his T-shirt that he was wearing by accident. That's when it went all bad, he jerked his head away from the sink and water from his hair was pouring everywhere. I said, "what's the matter", he said "you wet my shirt", I said "on accident, I'm sorry but we have to get the rest of the soap out of your hair". He was so mad he started hitting me hard with his towel. He started walking out of the kitchen, then I heard a loud bang and glass cracking, he was in the hallway, and he had broken a

911, Broken. **Give it to God!**

nice picture of a lady in a gold frame that I had got from my ex next door neighbors when we had just moved in. I was so upset and hurt. It felt like I had lost my child to something else. I ran over to the room next to the hallway where I always watch TV, the den, and I sat on the futon in there and started screaming and crying. He started to say, "I'm not going to the graduation ceremony today", I told him you need to go, I'll pick up the glass because I didn't want him to pick it up, but he was saying he'll pick it up. I insisted and went to get a bag and I started picking it up so that he didn't cut himself. I told him to please calm down and go rinse the conditioner out of your hair, because I was done at this point, and I wasn't going to touch him. We were also waiting on his dad to come and whoever he was bringing. His dad of course was running late like always. I was getting worried about that because I believe I mentioned before that he had to be there at 10am, everyone had a different time because of social distancing, I didn't want him to miss his time. I had got all the glass cleaned up and vacuumed the floor. I was still very shaken up behind all this and still very hurt, my son kept saying "mom, I'll get you another picture" but I was numb. Finally, his father pulls up with his girlfriend and I had to tell him what just happened and get him to talk Xman into finishing getting dressed. It was a real task. I was so upset I told his father to just take Xman up to the school before he's too late. I didn't go then, I still had to calm down. It was about 10 minutes before I left, and I got in my car, and went up there. When I was getting ready to park in the parking lot, I saw Xman's dad drive and honk at me going down the street, so I followed him. He pulled up in the Walgreens parking lot down the street. I asked him what happened, he told me there was hardly anyone there, so Xman was up first, and that they took pictures, and that he would send me the pictures. I missed it, everything. His father said it was about five minutes long and that was it, very disappointing for everyone, but the good thing about it is that Xman got his certificate. I drove home. I had bought a camera for the ceremony so I could have pictures of everything. When we came back home, I took a picture of Xman still in his attire in the living room, he looked so nice. I was so proud of him, even though I was still upset about the fight. See you can love and dislike a person's ways sometimes, even

The Graduation

if it's your child, especially if it's chronic circumstances such as mine. I knew I had to forgive my son because that's what the Lord did for me. He forgave me on that Cross of all my craziness and sins and for everything we have done in life, which is a lot. Can you even imagine some of the stuff you did, and can you imagine how it was for the Lord on that Cross to have to take on the sins of the whole world, what He experienced? I know no one can, but Christ our Savior, and I so thank Him for that, or I would be doomed to hell! Thank you, Lord Jesus!

Xman was apologizing and like I said before, he offered to get another picture, at the time, I really wasn't feeling him. Meaning, a lot went through my mind, even though I knew I was going to eventually forgive him. I looked around the house and saw all the holes he made in the walls that had been patched, and painted over, and all of my pictures sitting in the corner of my living room that had been destroyed, and remembering all the horrific statements we had made to one another. It was more than enough. I thought to myself as soon as he's finished with all this graduation and the rest of his work that he's doing and has to turn in, that we might need to live in separate places. I felt like I just couldn't, and didn't want this to continue to happen, because I never knew when another flare up might occur.

Now, he was, like I said, still working on work from the school at home that had to be turned in at a certain time. I was the one to pick it up from the parking lot around the corner at his school and bring it back. It was best to drive through, he didn't have that much left to finish so I needed him to complete it and get his credit. He really only has one grade to work on because he has A's, B's and C's and one D-, that's the one he needs to bring up, the D-. As I said earlier, he must have been working on the 1st packet or some of those other grades wouldn't have changed. I think Xman just played me. He knows how to do Zoom on the computer and interact with his teachers on email. Xman had strong computer skills since around 2 years old. I was so thankful to see that there was only one grade that needed to come up for now because normally he's had all A's and B's, but because he's at a new school, his grades are a little off, it's OK for now. Thank you, Jesus! My emotional roller coaster could now slow down. I had also been praying periodically about this anyway. That's why we need to trust the Lord and keep the faith like Paul the Apostle said. When I saw his grades and saw how he had even brought up some of his grades since he had been out of school due to the virus, I went and got him a nice Bluetooth speaker that he'd been wanting. I also told him how proud I was of him and that I loved him.

I was speaking to my mother, Xman's grandmother, that he likes to talk to, and she said that she felt that Xman's self-esteem had been low. I had to put myself in his situation and look at the matter from a different standpoint. First off, he didn't have a normal or traditional graduation or prom due to the pandemic. He hasn't been able to really go anywhere while out of school, only to the store and back, or with me to pick up food at a curbside service or drive through, that's it, and work on his packets at home. What a life, right? If this were me at this age, a teen of 18 years old, I'd go crazy. I felt soooo bad about all the arguments we had and the things we said, and I told him how proud I was of him and that I loved him. I realize that's all that mattered was some recognition. That's what we as humans all need, encouragement. Things started to get better. I felt a lot better also from the Lord delivering me from the drugs and alcohol. Xman and I started to converse more, eating together more as well. As for now, the lawsuit against the school district that I was pursuing is on hold due to the Covid 19 Virus. The courts have rescheduled it down the line. We'll see how that unfolds later.

Xman still has the last packet to hand in by June 5th and the last day of school is on June 11th and that's a wrap. Today, Xman and I will be speaking to his caseworker from the school, and other staff members over the phone. We'll be going over his exit and making a plan for the best of his future. His caseworker at school had called me about a couple of weeks ago and told me about a program still at the same high school he had his graduation ceremony at called Connections. This program entails life skills and prepares you for the real world. We'll be speaking about that today, so we'll see what happens with it. We received a call from the caseworker and staff and were given different options about that program "Connections", but Xman said he didn't want to sign up for it, because he didn't want to go back to that school. However, the caseworker told me about a program that can help

The Graduation

him get his diploma, because at the graduation ceremony, he only got a certificate because he has 10 credits to make up. He needs to put a little more work in to get his diploma. The caseworker, Mrs. S., said this other program would help him get it done. Mrs. S. also said the program at the adult school was easier than a Junior College, it would be part-time, and he could do it from home. She gave me the name of the lady in charge. We need to make an appointment with her for Xman. I was told about a paid internship for Xman too. I know the Lord is working on our behalf. Thank you, Jesus! Xman hadn't gotten his yearbook yet, so I contacted his father because I needed him to fill out the app for the yearbook. Finally, he called me back. His father kept telling me to have Xman fill it out, sometimes he can be difficult. Xman was already upset with his dad because he wasn't calling him back. Now you know what I'm going to do don't you, because I don't want any strife. Yep, that's right, I'm going to take all this to The Father in prayer.

CHAPTER 25:

Effects of Covid

Yesterday was Shavuot, it's a Jewish holiday known as the Feast of Weeks and Pentecost in Hebrew, the Jewish High Holy Holiday celebrated and found in the book of Acts in the Bible. It's very important as a Christian to celebrate the High Holy Holidays of the Jewish people because not only does it bless you, but we can also recognize them as our holidays also, and it gives you an understanding of the Jewish people. I don't know about you, but it's been a blessing to me. This particular one is when the Holy Spirit came upon them and they began to speak in other tongues as the Spirit gave them utterance, read Acts 2:1-4 in the Bible. Matter of fact, keep reading so you can get a good understanding of it, it's crucial that you see it for yourself, so nobody can lie to you. I took Xman out that morning to eat down the street because they started opening up restaurants and different businesses, as long as we followed the guidelines. When we got there, they took our temperature and you had to wear a mask until you were served. The tables were also six feet apart from one another. Xman and I needed this time to bond and talk. He started telling me about how depressed he was and that he'd been contemplating suicide again. I thought everything had been okay with him because my mother had been talking to him periodically and she said he sounds happy and didn't seem to show any signs of depression. I don't know what's going on. After Xman brought up the subject, I asked him why did he feel like that? He started cursing at me and told me he was ready to leave. Then I asked him "do you not want to eat here"? and then he changed his mind, and said he wanted his food. He's confused, and I'm

911, Broken. **Give it to God!**

even getting confused too. Seems like he only does this with me. He might talk with other people, but he doesn't rare up to them like he does me. I take that back, because he's done it to defend me a couple of times, but I'm just saying, it gets out of hand at times. I told Xman while in the restaurant, you do the talking and I'll listen. That's when he still brought up the depression, suicide, etc. After listening for a while, I then told him "Everybody's going through something right now with this pandemic". I said, "you have to stop thinking so negatively". I told him "You see, they're starting to open up more businesses again and you'll be able to start doing more things in a while". I told him "I'm going to get you back in driver's training so you can get your license and you'll be going back to school soon too, you'll be meeting new people that are mature, that really want to learn and go to school". I also told him I was very proud of him because he's come so far. This all happened on Sunday and that Sunday evening, I had a handy man coming over to look at some things in my home that needed to be fixed, such as, the walls with holes, drawers, etc. This was because I had been contemplating moving, because the house I live in is beautiful and fairly new, with an open concept, but the walls are very thin, and the doors are hollow. This is why when Xman hits them he can just cave them in. I've got holes everywhere and the handyman that comes over has a professional background in fixing up houses. He has a lot of experience in some of the things that I need fixed. At the same time, I've been looking at houses and I've got my eye on one that has a pool house on the property with a shower in it that I thought would be great for Xman so he could have his own living quarters and start living more on his own also. He always tells me that I treat him like he's younger than what he is. This house I've been looking at is an older home with thick concrete walls that can't be broken. It also has a pool for the hot summers in the Central Valley of California. I of course prayed for the Lord's Will to be done in this matter about the home. Now later that Sunday evening as I was going to bed, Xman came in my room to talk. He was talking about the same things that he was talking about in the restaurant, and asked me if I hated him, and of course, I told him "NO! I don't hate you; I love you, you're my child". I told him to leave the past behind and start to focus on the future.

Effects of Covid

I told Xman to give me a hug, he did. Then very shortly after, he started to bring up more negativity and I got up and told him to go to his room. I told him I'm real tired, and I'm trying to get some rest because the handyman will be coming in the morning. He started coming towards me in my room and put his hands up as though he was going to do something to me. I was in fear for my life, I ran past him to the kitchen and got on the phone and told him I was going to call 911 if he came any closer to me. He kept screaming "I'm going to my room, but he would keep coming out of it like he wanted to keep arguing. I then called my mother and my daughter. I got on the phone with them, and they could hear us arguing, he also punched another hole in his bedroom door. I was at wits end. My daughter was screaming through the phone at him, and she also called my brother and Xman's father. I tried to call his father earlier, but when I spoke with him, he sounded very nonchalant, even though I told him what was happening. I didn't want to call the police on him because they had been dealing with protestors due to a police shooting and they were trying to keep the city under control, because it got real bad in a lot of different states due to racism allegations. When this sort of thing happens, everybody involved becomes hyped up. Anyway, my daughter got a hold of his father as well and he said he was in a city close by, and he would come pick up Xman. I went to Xman's room and told him to get ready for his father. He told me he would. Xman knew I was on the phone with the family, and we weren't playing. Early that next morning, about 1AM, his father dropped Xman back off. They called me when they got close and I told Xman before he comes in the house, he has to take some medicine, and I brought it to the door with me. I told him if he didn't take it, he wouldn't be able to come in, so when his dad pulled up with him, I met him at the door, and he took the pills for anxiety, and I had to take them too. My anxiety level was so high that the next day I had a real bad headache. The next day Xman had a phone appointment with his psychiatrist Dr. B. which was good. I needed to speak to his doctor myself and let him know what had happened the night before, to get some advice also. The doctor, when I told him what had transpired the night before, told me to have Xman take the medication he had prescribed for him or otherwise, he told me I might want to think about sending him to a group home. I remembered that night I had to call the prayer line and ask them to pray about Xman's dad to come, and he did show up. Xman did take those other meds before he came in the house to calm down. I did have some hope. In my son's case, he really needs help with his temper, you never know when he'll pop off. I'm looking for a big testimony from the both of us.

Yesterday the handyman came over to fix the holes in the wall and he told me I had to get two new doors, one for the hallway and one for Xman's room because they were unfixable. I remembered I had put in an offer for that other house I saw with the pool and back house. I called my real estate lady, and she told me someone else got it, they had a higher offer. I was a little upset, but I remembered what I prayed and asked the Lord. I asked Him to let His Will be done. Evidently, that was not His Will. I have to move on. I know the Lord has something even greater than that for me. I just have to trust and know that He will do it. I received a keychain from Jewish Voice Ministries that said on it "be still and know that I am God", Psalms 45:10 and in the Jewish vocabulary, there's no such word for coincidence, to me, that means it's meant for whatever happens to happen. Yesterday I waited on the handyman that my real estate lady referred to me, but he never showed up. I called her up and let her know that he was a no show and she told me she would give him a call, she called him but no answer. I called also and left a message. He never called me back. I called a second time, and someone picked up the phone, and just hung up in my face. I thought to myself "is this guy hiding something from me, is he on drugs or what". I paid him the day before, a nice sum of money for what he fixed in the house, and even cleaned up behind him. I'm trying to get everything fixed in the house so I can put it on the market to sell. I also was told by my real estate lady, Ms. L., that the other house that I had bid on, with the pool accepted another offer, so that was out. She also told me she had a couple of other houses to look at and I did want to go look at them. At first, I told her I only wanted the first house and if I couldn't get that one, I wasn't wanting to look for anymore, but I ended up going with her that afternoon. Ms. L. came a little early and I showed her the work in my home that the handyman hadn't finished.

Effects of Covid

Looking around she saw all the holes that had been made by Xman, and as I had her go over everything, she kept saying "another hole". I told her "Yes", and I even have to replace two doors that aren't fixable. Even the real estate lady could feel me, and how I needed a place at least with solid walls and doors so that they wouldn't be easy to damage, and/or separate quarters on the same grounds like, a guest house for Xman.

Xman and I are about to go to the mall, it finally reopened. I had been out running errands all that morning. I had just got back to the house, Xman had been awake. When I came in, he was asking me to take him to the mall, it was a beautiful day, mind you, this is in June, I'm speaking about, and where we're at normally by now we're in the upper 90's to triple digits. This day it was in the 80's, just perfect with a breeze. I told Xman I was tired from running errands and I wanted to rest a little. I also told him I would take him to the bus stop because at first, I felt like taking him, but I overexerted myself and since it was such a nice day, I thought he would enjoy the bus ride. He started revving up, the same old thing, cursing, calling me out of my name. We started arguing because I was heated that he disrespected me. I really shouldn't of said anything back, but I wasn't thinking at the time, just reacting. I thought to myself, another out of control episode about to happen. Xman was getting ready to make some ramen noodles, he had already put them in the pot, all of a sudden, he took the pot and threw the noodles up against the kitchen wall. I finally got a grip on myself, went out in the garage to cool off. Then, I came back and told him "OK, get dressed and I'll take you". I know you're wondering why I'm still going to take him, and am I crazy, well, if you were in my shoes, you wouldn't even ask. At the same time, I was thinking to myself, how much I had had it and the devil was in one ear telling me "Hey, you're only human, you're allowed to make mistakes". Now remember, I believe I told you that I had been sober now for almost a month or so now. I was thinking too much and hard about how I was going to relieve this anxiety I'm having while Xman was getting ready. I called up an ex-dealer I knew, and he told me he would be at home. I was contemplating going over there, and right now it didn't take much to convince myself. I also talked to Xman and told him, in order for me to take

143

him, he'd have to calm down before getting in the car, because the first sign of any anger, and I'm going to forget the whole thing. Beside the devil, I was also convincing myself that I needed something strong to relax, which was a lie from the pit of hell! I got Xman in the car, he had calmed down, I then proceeded to the mall. When we got there, you could clearly see that the mall was ready for business. Everybody and their mother was there, I guess everyone was so tired of having to stay in due to the Covid 19 Virus, and being isolated. They couldn't wait to get some kind of outlet. Xman asked me to pull over by one of the entrances where he saw the rest of the crowd going into and I asked him if he had his phone and keys, he said yes and got out. I was so relieved. I felt like a ton of bricks had just been lifted from my back and I could finally breathe again, but that still didn't stop me from wanting to medicate and get something for being stressed, even though he was gone. I was telling myself to take a day off mentally. It wasn't right but I was at a no care crisis in my mind. I ended up going by that guy's house and picked up the meds. I thought about going over a couple of people's houses, but then I thought, I didn't want to go too far and get back in contact with those old acquaintances that were doing the same thing as I was about to do, and like the Word says, "don't make others stumble". I had enough sense not to do that but believe me it crossed my mind, thank God I didn't. I went home and started drinking and medicating and I felt relief for a minute. I had started calling my mother and other family members that I hadn't been speaking to for a while and reaching out. I really didn't have any business calling them under the influence, but every time I got that stuff, I wanted to talk. Although sometimes I bet, they knew what was going on with me. Then, after a few hours, I could see my son walking up the street coming towards the house as I was sitting in the garage looking that way. I thought to myself, here comes trouble. I really wanted him to stay a little longer, but I did think also that maybe he feels better since he got a break. When he came in, I had asked him how was it, he said, "OK, but a lot of the stores I wanted to go to were closed due to the virus". He went in his room and closed the door. I was still drinking. Later that evening we had another argument. This time, I got in touch with his father, and he also called Xman up.

Effects of Covid

He told me that his father was on the way to pick him up. I was at the time, beside myself. I called my mother and daughter and they also called Xman's dad, and they told me that he was coming. I was crying out of control and exhausted. After my mother and daughter heard how I was sounding, they didn't want to wait any longer and they were also on their way too. Xman's dad was supposed to be on his way.

CHAPTER 26:

Spiritual Warfare & Broken

As I was waiting, I took some more meds, finally his father got there and picked him up. The meds kicked in and I had a horrifying experience! I felt like darkness overshadowed me, and it felt like the world was coming to an end, that's the best way to describe it. Fear overtook me. Anxiety came in as soon as the car drove off. This must of happened in no less than 20 minutes, the sky looked dark. I felt all alone, my heart was racing out of control, it felt like Jesus was on his way, but I felt as if I was left behind. It was terrifying and there was nothing I could do. I started walking back through the garage to the door to go in, but I didn't really want to go in, more fear came over me. The garage got dark, I felt this was it. As I started to come through this horrific vision, I started thanking God and at the same time, realizing if I didn't get my act together, this could literally happen to me. I don't want to be left behind. I want my family, and myself and loved ones, to go with Jesus. I also want to be sober, joyful and at peace with God. People play around and say things like they'll be partying in hell but, no they won't, and they'll see all their friends, not so. The Bible describes hell as a place of loneliness, no God, no friends, total darkness, agonizing, gnashing and grinding of teeth, and eternal death spiritually, and unquenchable fire forever. Who in their right mind wants to live and get tormented day and night forever? I put some scripture down to read about hell, and I bet it will change a lot of minds about wanting to go, Psalms 55:15, Proverbs 23:14, Matthew 18:9, Luke 12:5, James 3:6, this is real.

Changing the subject, now I was waiting on my daughter and mother and grandkids, the two girls, to come in and I needed to get myself together, because I had had it. I was exhausted, my mind was out of whack, my nerves were bad, I needed Jesus! I also needed to see my family; I was tired of dealing with all of this alone. I know I have God, but as a human, I had lost it. I snapped and I needed to see some familiar faces, and even the Lord put it upon my family's heart to come to see me. I couldn't wait to see them, now on the other hand, Xman could. He didn't know how things were going to unfold. Finally, I got the call they were close. I was finally coming down from all the meds I took. I was angry with myself for breaking my sobriety that I wanted so much to have. I was broken and extremely hurt. It was crucial that I saw people who cared for me because no one where I was living, truly cared I felt, and most of the ones I knew weren't good for my sobriety except for the people at the church that was now closed due to the Covid 19 virus. I was really reaching. I had become isolated like my son and that can make you weird and your thoughts even worst if you let them, and that's just what happened, I should have been in more prayer, because this is the outcome when you don't put God first.

CHAPTER 27:

Hope

My daughter called me, and I went to go meet her, she got a little turned around. I just didn't want her to get lost so I suggested we meet at a nearby gas station. When I pulled up, I didn't recognize her, my daughter had a new jeep before, but this was a pretty reddish car. They honked the horn at me and waved for me to see them, I was elated with happiness. When we got to the house everyone was tired, so we talked for a while, not too long. Xman was in his room waiting on his father to pick him up. Finally, his father showed up and we all went to bed. Xman got home late so no one had a chance to speak with him that evening. The next day my daughter and I went to the store to buy groceries early that morning. We wanted to barbecue that day for our dinner. We bought McDonald's for breakfast so that we didn't have to cook twice. When we got back the grandkids were still lying down and my mother in the other room got up to see what we had bought. I had told her we didn't have to cook this morning because we bought take-out. After a while I knocked on Xman's door to ask him what were his plans for the day, and he told me that his father might be coming back over to pick him up. My daughter got the kids up to eat breakfast and she asked me if I thought Xman would want to go to the mall with them. I told her that he might be going with his dad that day. I know your probably wondering why I said his dad, well that's because my daughter's dad, my ex, passed away when she was about nine years old, and their fathers are different. Back to the mall question... no one pressed the issue after I said he was going with his dad, also, knowing he'd been acting up so bad and the two girls, my granddaughters, really weren't too sure how to approach him. We all kind of fell back when it came to him at the time. To my surprise, my daughter was very cool about the whole matter, and I thought to myself she probably wants to make peace, because she hadn't seen him for a long time. This was very hard for her, knowing her situation, because she was six months pregnant, and I didn't want her to get upset. It all worked out for the best, Xman went with his dad, and she went to the mall with the girls. I stayed with my mother and relaxed and we had some time to catch up and bond. After a few hours my daughter got back with the girls and later that day, coming towards evening, Xman came in. He went straight to his room, didn't say much because I guess he figured we had been talking about the blow-up incident anyway, and I know he probably felt a little embarrassed about his behavior. I had showed my mother and daughter all the holes in the walls that needed to be repaired also, the doors that needed to be replaced. You know I had been contemplating on selling the house anyway. I was tired of having to keep fixing it up. Xman needed his own quarters outside of the home and I had been speaking to a real estate agent about moving and finding me something, I had mentioned this earlier, something with a backhouse or guesthouse, whichever, a separate dwelling.

Now that Sunday, the girls and my mother had to get back to Pasadena, Ca., that is about 3 ½ hours from me, so that my daughter could get ready for work that next day. Xman had calmed down. I know my mother finally talked to him, and let him know that he better not break or destroy anything else in the house, or there would be stiff consequences. My brother, Xman's uncle, also had left messages on Xman's phone as well as my daughter. I believe he was getting the point. Before they left, the girls, my granddaughters, finally went in his room and he seemed to be very cool and quiet. I'd been praying for the Holy Spirit to convict him and I know He did because when they left, he really acted different, like he was convicted. Praise God!

The next week I got a call from my Pastor's wife, she told me that they were going to reopen the church, Praise God! They had gotten word it was okay to do so as long as they went by the guidelines of social distancing and masks and also, checking for symptoms such as fever and coughing. I was

Hope

so thankful. The following Sunday Xman and I went back, and it was awesome. Xman really wasn't into it this time, but it didn't matter to me because I know God was working it all out. After we left, I bought something to eat while we were out, so I didn't have to cook, and we went home. The message that Sunday was in the Book of Daniel, about the three Hebrew young men, that were put in the fire because they wouldn't bow down to the statue of Nebuchadnezzar, and that there was a fourth man walking around in the fire with them, which looked like the Son of God, which we all know, it was Jesus. They came out of the fire not even smelling like smoke, and alive, after the fire was put up seven times hotter, and even the guard who was by the fire, died because it was so hot, just being on the outside of it. With the Lord, all things are possible, and we all know that was a miracle that those guys didn't die and even made King Nebuchadnezzar a believer. It felt so good to go back to church, it made my faith stronger, and I felt more at peace knowing the Lord is working it all out. Just to be around believers, and praising the Lord, helps all the time, it gives you hope. Thank you, Lord for your grace and mercy.

The next week things went a little better even though everyone had left. I started back on looking for houses, writing and getting back in focus. Now you know of course, the devil was mad we made it to church, I could care less. I told myself I'm riding with God! and nothing's going to stop me even if I mess up, I'm going to get right back up and keep riding. I love the Lord, He is my everything and without Him, I can do nothing. I started seeing a change in Xman's behavior. I had told the Pastor's wife a little about what had happened during the time the church had been closed. She told me that she would be lifting us up in prayer and also, the following week seemed to go a lot better. Xman hadn't broken anything, we even started to bond more by communicating at breakfast and throughout the days. That's why it's good to have a support team, and that's why God wants us to have fellowship with other believers. It all makes sense to me now. Xman started up most of our conversations and I didn't interrupt him either. I'd sit back and let him finish venting or just talk. I knew the Lord had taken over the reigns because I surrendered it all to Him. Xman even started to ask me if he could do stuff instead of just telling me. I could clearly see the miracle evolve. He even started doing his chores on his own and coming out of the room more, even leaving his door cracked, he never did that. Now, I'm not saying that we agreed on everything, but I saw it all coming together slowly and the hand of the Lord was involved. The Lord was waiting on me to give it to Him, like I was supposed to do a long time ago, because only Him and Him alone could work this out. I had to fall back and let God be God, that was never my job and when I let go, He helped me.

The next week I got back Xman's grades from school, and I was so proud to see that the Lord had been behind the scenes working on Xman, because his grades had come up in all the classes that they were down in, Praise God! When Xman told me he was doing his work in the room, he actually was and I was elated to know that, with joy. On his report card he got A's and B's and a couple of C's, no D's or F's, thank you Jesus! and I picked up his Certificate of Completion as well. I told my son how proud of him I was and that I knew he could do it. His confidence went up. I told my mother, and daughter, and other family members about it also. See, all the time the Lord was wanting for me to stop trying to do His job for Him, that's all. We as humans think we know it all sometimes, and that we have the power to work it all out, wrong. We need the Lord in everything we do. He is our provider, our strength, our peace, all the Fruits of the Spirit, if we just let Him do His job, it will all be well. In Galatians, Chapter 5:22-23, you can read about the Fruits of the Spirit. I even received a key chain from a Jewish Rabbi believer that says "be still and know that I am God", Psalm 46:10, I had to be still. Nothing on earth will ever be perfect unless the Lord our God makes it that way. We can't in the flesh do that, only Jesus. I don't expect for the trials and tribulations to go away, because we have seasons of the good, bad, and the ugly. All I know is when we surrender to the Lord, He can make those crooked ways straight, and knock out the kinks, if you will. The Lord can also put a period where there's a doubt or question.

To change subjects, this Sunday, our Pastor even asked for prayer for his son to turn him to God. At first I was a little shocked, but you see, even Pastors are human and we can't expect their situations to be perfect like Jesus.

Hope

I don't know why when he first said it that I was so shocked, because I should have known nobody's perfect, and we all fall short sometimes. That's why the Lord gave us options like prayer to recognize that we need Him in our lives because if we could do it all ourselves, we wouldn't need Him. I feel it's just a reminder. I did pray for my Pastor's son and mine as well. I love the fact that the Pastor was so humble about it and wasn't afraid to let us know, that he also is human and not above anyone else. I really loved to know that it let me know that I was in a good church, one who believes that we all need Christ as well. This Sunday Xman wasn't really into it at all, I would glance over at him occasionally whenever the Pastor had asked us to sing and clap along or take a moment and Praise the Lord, and Xman wouldn't do it.

At the very end of the service, they always have an altar call, and also ask if there are any prayer requests or praise reports. One lady there raised her hand and gave one, I also raised my hand and gave another but it wasn't about Xman, it was for any of my family members that weren't into Christ, that they would turn to Him, and repent and receive salvation. After that we would give our tithes and offerings, then we would get dismissed. Xman and I left, got in the car and he seemed to have an attitude. I asked him what was wrong, and he told me that I didn't ask for prayer for him, and I asked him, what about? He told me that he mentioned to me that he'd been depressed, and having too many bad thoughts about his past. I then told him that he could have asked for prayer himself, because I had so much on my mind, I'd forgotten. I also told him that if there's anything that's bothering him, do like the rest of the people in the church, and let Pastor know, he'd be more than happy to pray with him, that's what he's here for. I told him I can't remember his stuff and mine too, it's just too much. It's what you would call an overload. Xman then told me he felt a little shy to say anything. Then he got upset and he started to say things that were real foul like, "I don't want to go back to church" and some other things I won't discuss. I told him to stop getting so offended when someone is trying to talk to him about what he has a question about, and hear them out. You might understand that they care about your situation, give them a chance. He's told me several times that he feels I don't care, and I have reassured him several times that I love him,

153

911, Broken. **Give it to God!**

and he's my only son and I'll do what I can to help him if it's in my power. I love my son but I dislike some of his ways and I'm entitled to say that if they aren't right. This is why I stay in prayer. It also goes for me too.

CHAPTER 28:

The Power of God's Word!

I know there's people that have dealt with me, they love me, but might not like some of my ways either, no one's excluded. This is why we need Christ, to redirect us in the right way to go when we mess up. This is another reason why prayer is so important, keeping you focused on the right things in life and to make good sound decisions. Another book in the Bible that really helped me was the Book of Proverbs that Solomon wrote, it's the wisdom book. It helped me to start writing this book, also gave me better wisdom, understanding and knowledge, that's what we all need to succeed in life. It also gave me a lot of creative thoughts and ideas. I've heard testimonies from million and billionaire's that said the Book of Proverbs helped them by reading it to prosper, God's Word is powerful.

To change the subject, even though Xman said what he said about church, that he didn't want to go back to it was because he wanted to be heard and he was reaching out. That doesn't mean that I'm going to stop loving him. I'm going to stay in prayer for my son and that's all I can do, and listen to him more, because like I said before, he's been doing a lot better. I believe it has a lot to do with not being able to do much since the Virus. This week, while eating together, he's been opening up a lot and I've been just listening and occasionally, putting in my input after getting a clear understanding of what he's trying to say. The Lord has been guiding me, and I believe also, the Lord has put a guard over my tongue so that I won't say the wrong things. Seems like it's really working out a lot better. Thank you, Jesus! Also, Xman hasn't put any holes in the walls lately, and

911, Broken. **Give it to God!**

we really haven't had any heated arguments, disagreements yes, but nothing like before. I anointed Xman's pillow and the house and myself with the oil I got from one of the ministries I listen to. The Lord has heard my cry. I pray for everyone who reads this book, that they can see that the negative can turn into a positive through Christ our Lord, and I know that God is in control, and I trust Him to see a thing through. In life, nothing will be perfect because we go through seasons of good and bad, trials and tribulations it's called. That's why we have to have that faith in knowing that we need the Lord in everything we do. that's the only way we will succeed. Like he told us in Jeremiah, 29:11-12, "For I know the thoughts I think towards you says the Lord, thoughts of peace and not of evil, to give you a future and a hope. Then you will call upon Me and go and pray to Me, and I will listen to you", out of the New King James Version Bible.

I also pray that any parent of a child fighting Autism, learn that the only way I made it this far was through Christ, and trusting Him. There were times when I just wanted to throw in the towel, but Jesus kept me from giving up, and only Him. God has provided for us, giving me homes, health, wisdom and strength to keep it moving forward, Glory to God! and if He can do it for me, He will do it for you. We're all a work in progress and it says in Romans 3:23, New King James Version, "for all have sinned and fallen short of the glory of God", and if you would like to give God a try repeat this prayer aloud. Romans 10:9-10 says, that "if you confess with your mouth the Lord Jesus and believe in your heart that God has raised Him from the dead, you will be saved. For with the heart one believes unto righteousness, and with the mouth confession is made unto salvation". Say this with sincerity, and the Lord will hear and receive you as His own. May God bless you for the rest of your life. Glory to the Lord for allowing me to be able to bless others with the info I was able to share to whoever reads this book. Be blessed.

P.S. Pray for the peace of Israel, for it say's in Genesis 12:3, "I will bless those who bless you, and I will curse him who curses you!" I would like to make a suggestion, and that is to read the Book of Proverbs from the Bible to help anyone that needs wisdom, understanding and knowledge because

The Power of God's Word!

that's what inspired me to write this book and also a lot to do with what I wrote. This book also gave me wisdom on making the right decisions in my walk with God, kids and other circumstances, and the whole Bible gave me instructions that I needed for my walk through life. Through all our trials and tribulations, we always need that Godly wisdom. I pray for all my readers to receive insight in learning on how to deal with this complicated and frustrating disease known as Autism, and I pray Jeremiah 29:11 over you as well that says "for I know the thoughts that I think towards you, says the Lord, thoughts of peace and not of evil, to give you a future and a hope". These are crucial times, and we all need God's blessings. By the way, Xman just made up his credits he was lacking to get his Diploma, and he just graduated from High School! Praise God! Now he's talking about pursuing college or work. The Lord is dealing with me also. I just got Baptized on August 14, 2022, and rededicated my life to the Lord, and the Lord has broken off the dependency of drugs and alcohol off my life, thank you, Jesus! It helps to be in a good Bible believing church as well, to fellowship, and have support. God bless you!

Family & Supporters

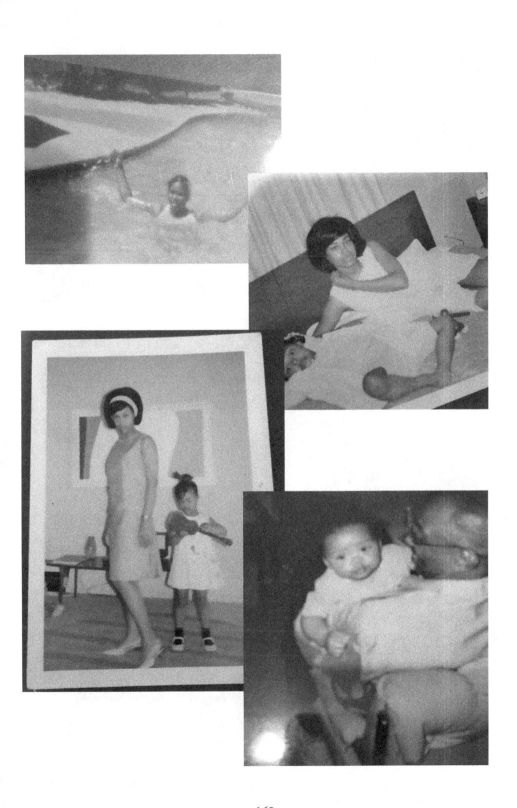

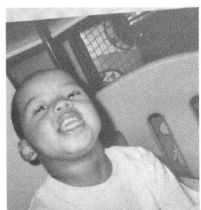

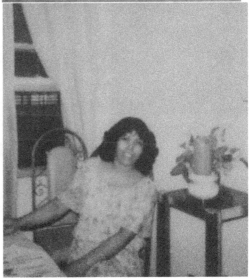